PERGAMON INTERNATIONAL LIBRARY
of Science, Technology, Engineering and Social Studies
*The 1000-volume original paperback library in aid of education,
industrial training and the enjoyment of leisure*
Publisher: Robert Maxwell, M.C.

INTRODUCTION TO THE THEORY
AND CONTEXT OF ACCOUNTING

£3.95

INTRODUCTION TO THE THEORY AND CONTEXT OF ACCOUNTING

SECOND EDITION

BY

ROY SIDEBOTHAM

PERGAMON PRESS

Oxford · New York · Toronto
Sydney · Paris · Frankfurt

U.K.	Pergamon Press Ltd., Headington Hill Hall, Oxford OX3 0BW, England
U.S.A.	Pergamon Press Inc., Maxwell House, Fairview Park, Elmsford, New York 10523, U.S.A.
CANADA	Pergamon of Canada Ltd., 75 The East Mall, Toronto, Ontario, Canada
AUSTRALIA	Pergamon Press (Aust.) Pty. Ltd., 19a Boundary Street, Rushcutters Bay, N.S.W. 2011, Australia
FRANCE	Pergamon Press SARL, 24 rue des Ecoles, 75240 Paris, Cedex 05, France
FEDERAL REPUBLIC OF GERMANY	Pergamon Press GmbH, 6242 Kronberg-Taunus, Pferdstrasse 1, Federal Republic of Germany

First edition 1965

Second edition 1970

Reprinted 1973, 1974, 1975, 1976, 1977

Library of Congress Catalog Card No. 77-103594

Printed in Great Britain by Biddles Ltd., Guildford, Surrey

ISBN 0 08 015619 3 (flexicover)

Contents

Objective

THERE are many books on the methodology of accounting; neither teachers nor students experience any difficulty in finding good books on the technical aspects of the subject. Additionally, in recent years there has been a good deal of writing on accounting theory, but this has mostly been of interest to advanced students.

Accordingly, professional examination and university undergraduate students often learn accounting solely as a technical exercise in the application of double-entry recording to a variety of commercial enterprises, without related study of the history, theory and environment of accounting.

This book is meant as a supplement to existing texts, offering students, early in their reading, some appreciation of the context, potential and limitations of accounting, and serving as a base for outward-looking development in more advanced work. Some areas of accounting theory are, as yet, controversial, and though an attempt has been made to present a balanced view, it would not be practical in a short book designed for introductory students to give a comprehensive treatment. It is, however, hoped that thought will be stimulated, and a bibliography has been provided in Appendix B to facilitate further exploration of the subject.

Introduction to the Theory and Context of Accounting is intended for use in class work with first or second year students in colleges and universities, in conjunction with other books dealing with the technology of financial and management accounting. To assist teachers and students, a series of discussion topics, following from the text, has been appended to each chapter except Chapter 9. Introductory students are advised to read Appendix A on the basic ideas of double-entry before tackling the main text.

Victoria University   R.S.
Wellington New Zealand

Acknowledgements

THOUGH this second edition of *Introduction to the Theory and Context of Accounting* differs materially from the first, it is built on the work of those who contributed to the earlier book, notably Dr. G. Fogelberg, Mr. P. C. Byers, Mr. E. G. Freeman and Mr. J. S. Stacey. For their continuing contribution I am grateful.

Chapters 4 and 9 of the present edition are contributed by Professor R. J. Chambers of the University of Sydney, and my thanks are due to him for permission to reproduce his writings.

Professor H. D. W. Barton and Mr. P. A. Griffin of the Victoria University of Wellington have read the manuscript and made many useful suggestions, and Professor R. S. Gynther of the University of Queensland commented on the draft of Chapter 8. Whilst Professor Barton, Mr. Griffin and Professor Gynther do not share responsibility for the book, I am grateful for their help.

R.S.

PART I HISTORY

CHAPTER 1

The Origins of Modern Accounting

ACCOUNTING is sometimes spoken of as being a new subject, a recent introduction to educational curricula, a product of the commercial and industrial activity of the modern age. Such is far from being the case. Whenever and wherever economic affairs have progressed beyond the most elementary conditions of production and exchange, systems of account have appeared. Inventories, wage lists, tax assessments and accounts as old as 4500 B.C. have been found, [1] and there are plenty of Egyptian, Greek, Roman, early European and medieval accounting records in existence. At each stage of development, men have used accounting, according to their needs, and within the limits of the recording and analysing techniques known to them, to enumerate and control assets, as a reporting device for agents, stewards and tax gatherers, as evidence of trade, for the control of production and the management of business.

Double-entry

Though there are plenty of records of earlier accounting, modern methodology began with the development of double-entry in the thirteenth and fourteenth centuries. Accounting by double-entry has substantial advantages over the unco-ordinated recording methods used earlier—it is firmly based on the dual nature of each business transaction—for each debtor there must be a creditor, for each payer a receiver, for each seller a purchaser.

[1] See, for instance, O. R. Keister, Commercial record keeping in Ancient Mesopotamia, *Accounting Review,* April 1963, p.361.

It provides the basis for the comprehensive and orderly recording of all the financial aspects of the transactions of a business, affords a means of proof of accurate accounting through the equality of total debit and credit entries, and by the integration in the ledger of personal, real and nominal accounts, provides material for the development of statements of profit and loss, and of equity, assets, and liabilities. It has been described[1] as " ... born of the same spirit as the systems of Galileo and Newton. ... Using the same means as these, it orders the phenomena into an elegant system, and it may be described as the first cosmos built up on the basis of mechanistic thought", yet it is unlikely to have been an invention, the conception of any single scholar or merchant. More likely it was a natural development of earlier recording systems under the stimulus of the growth of trade generated in the Mediterranean by the Crusades, and by the mercantile activities of the Italian City States during the Renaissance.

Twelfth-century business records were very simple in form, amounting to little more than memorandum accounts of short-term partnerships engaged in mercantile ventures, yet they established a basic idea of accounting—the separation of the records of a business from those of the owners' personal estates. In the thirteenth century, two developments had their impact on accounting; the increase in credit transactions and the growing use of agencies, often in foreign cities, to deal with the local sale of exported merchandise, and the more complex records required would lead naturally to the recognition of the dual effect of transactions. Thus money received from an agent would appear twice in the books of the principal, once as a credit in the agent's personal account, and again, but as a debit in the cash record, and money lent would cause equal entries to be made in a debtor's account and in the cash account in the books of the lender. By 1322 the del Bene company of Florence, which was engaged in importing, processing and selling cloth, had an effective set of

[1] W. Sombart, *Der Moderne Kapitalismus* (6th edn., Munich and Leipzig, 1924), vol. 2, part 1, p.119.

records which, if they did not achieve full double-entry, certainly recognised simultaneous debit and credit entries in some circumstances.

By the fourteenth century Italian merchants and manufacturers had developed substantial industrial activities, and had established trading branches throughout the known world; the Florentine Peruzzi company, for instance, had branches in Avignon, Barletta, Bruges, Sardinia, Cyprus, London, Majorca, Naples, Paris, Pisa, Rhodes, Sicily and Venice. As the century progressed, the City States became very wealthy. They created banking and other financial institutions, organised trade throughout the Middle East, and their economic and political influence extended from Scandinavia to India. It is from this century, and from Italy, that we have the earliest known set of accounts fully satisfying the requirements of the double-entry system, those of the Stewards of the Commune of Genoa for the year 1340. In their accounts each debit has a corresponding credit, there are separate expense accounts, and the Commune Account serves as a capital account, to which the balances on all expense and revenue accounts were closed at the year-end.

The gradual development of double-entry is well illustrated by the records of Francesco di Marco Datini, a Tuscan merchant-banker, many of whose records from around 1335 to 1410 are preserved in Prato. Though, in the early stages of Datini's business, the books were kept by single entry, double-entry was certainly in use by 1390. Datini's balance sheet on 31 January 1399 contains entries such as Debtors, Creditors, Balances with Foreign Correspondents, Balances with Branches, Goods in Stock, Bad Debts, Reserves for Accrued Taxes and Contingencies, Owners' Equity and, perhaps most significant of all, "Untraced Error in Casting the Balance".[1] Accrual accounting, depreciation provisions, and the creation of reserves, all of which were used by Datini, antedate 1400.

[1] Datini Archives, Prato (Tuscany), No. 1165. The balance sheet is illustrated in Raymond de Roover, *Accounting Prior to Luca Pacioli* at pp.142–3 in Littleton and Yamey, *Studies in the History of Accounting* London, 1956.

The Medici Bank of Florence, which was founded in 1397, provides another interesting example. Besides considerable banking business conducted in Florence and through branches in other Italian cities and major trading centres abroad, the Bank operated several manufacturing establishments. Each branch, and each factory, was a separate entity, with separate partners, capital, and accounts, though the Medici family had a controlling interest in each of them; an organisation not dissimilar from the modern holding company and subsidiaries. The Medici Bank used double-entry—any lesser system would have been inadequate for the range and volume of its transactions, and there were reciprocal or controlling accounts between the branches. A copy of each branch's balance sheet was sent each year to Florence, and was subject to audit, mainly as a control over ageing or doubtful debts. The Medici accounts contained provisions for accrued wages, bad debts, and contingencies, and these provisions were on occasions used to correct overstatements of profits in previous years.

Luca Pacioli

The first known published book on accountancy was the work of a Franciscan monk, Luca Pacioli, a scholar of standing, who taught in the universities at Milan, Pavia, Florence, Pisa and Bologna, besides, at the invitation of Pope Leo X, at the Academy in Rome. Pacioli was a typical early Renaissance scholar, a friend of Pope Julius II and of Leonardo da Vinci, and, though primarily a mathematician, his interests extended to painting, architecture, sculpture and military science. He had some experience of commerce, mostly gained in Venice, and, in 1494 he included in his book *Summa di Aritmetica Geometria Proportioni et Proportionalita—Everything about Arithmetic, Geometry and Proportion*, a section on accounting entitled De Computis et Scriptures, which was republished separately in 1504 in Tuscany under the title *La Scuola Perfetta dei Mercanti—The Perfect School of Merchants*.

Pacioli made no claim to be the inventor of double-entry, indeed he states in the *Summa* that he was describing methods which had been used in Venice for over 200 years. He refers to three books, each of equal importance: the waste book or memorial, the journal and the ledger. The sequence he describes begins with an inventory of the "personal belongings and household goods, estate, etc." of the merchant. Individual transactions are then recorded in the memorial, as they occur, by "the owner, his agents, or assistants". Care must be taken to record transactions in full. "No point must be omitted: if possible put down also what words were exchanged during the transaction." The memorial constitutes a written record of transactions as they took place. No special form is suggested and no attempt at standardising the presentation of this basic material is made.

The entries in the inventory and the memorial are transferred to the journal, for which a particular form is advocated. The journal entry must distinguish between debit and credit. "At the commencement of each entry is always put the expression debit because the debtor must always be described first; and immediately after, the creditor." The entries are recorded in the journal in the order in which the events or transactions occurred.

From the journal, accounts are written up in the ledger, which should have an index or table showing the position and page number of each individual account. When posting, each journal entry must be "posted twice: i.e., once to the debit and the other to the credit". The date of particular entries must not be placed over them, as in the journal, but opposite them on the margin. Accounts of various transactions and the manner in which they should be treated are illustrated by Pacioli. He deals with entries in the books required when the merchant keeps a branch store away from his house, or when he has money on deposit in a bank, or when travelling, or for brokerage, barter or partnership.

With regard to the calculation of profit, Pacioli writes: "There are certain accounts which one may not wish to transfer (to the next accounting period) such as expenses and income. These accounts should therefore be closed to profit and loss account." He deals with the balance on profit and loss account as follows: "Having seen your gain or loss by this account, you will then follow by closing and transferring it to capital accounts, wherein the beginning of your affairs you entered therein the inventory. . . . "

Pacioli and the Accounting Practice of His Time

Though it is probable that the rather simple system of accounting described in Pacioli's thesis was in fairly general use in fifteenth-century Italy, there is no doubt that more refined methods were known in the counting houses from which the great firms of the time were run. Pacioli does not refer to cost accounting, though the Medici account books show that a crude form of this type of analysis was in use in 1531. Further, the records of del Bene in the middle of the fifteenth century show two sets of books, one dealing with the industrial side of the business and ascertaining the cost of products made, and the other dealing with mercantile affairs. It is clear that some form of cost analysis was used in Pacioli's time, yet there is no mention of this in the *Summa*. Nor does Pacioli mention other contemporary techniques. For example, Datini prepared accounts which separated in different columns foreign currencies, and compared them with the value of home currencies at the date of the transaction, leading to the recognition of differences in value between foreign currencies and local moneys as profits or losses on exchange dealings. Although Pacioli dealt with exchange calculations in the Fourth Section of the *Summa*, which was concerned with money and exchange, he only touches on the accounting aspects of the problem. When describing journal entries made for foreign payments he states: "You shall mention what kind of moneys you draw and remit and their values." No attempt is made to isolate the profit or loss on exchange transactions within the double-entry system. Subsidiary books and controlling and reciprocal accounts in the ledger were known fifteenth-century practices, yet Pacioli's *Summa* contains no record of such accounts.

He refers to internal check, but not to auditing, yet the audit of balance sheets was a standard procedure in the Medici Bank.

Pacioli's work, therefore, is not a comprehensive treatment of known accounting methods. Rather is it a description of the common practice of fifteenth-century merchants. Yet underlying the practices he described lies a conceptual basis for accountancy, a series of unstated assumptions which the early merchants applied when they formulated rules for the extraction of accounting information from the environment.

Pacioli clearly recognised double-entry. In Chapter 34 of the *Summa* he states: " . . . and therefore never must an amount be entered in credit which is not also entered in the same amount in debit. . . . " Secondly, he advocated yearly balancing of accounts, although the procedure was not mandatory, as there were no regulations of law or conventions of society to require it. Chapter 29 of the *Summa:* "It is always a good thing to balance books each year, particularly for those who trade in partnership with others; as the proverb says—'frequent accounts favour long friendships'." Unfortunately there has been some confusion on this point, involving the question whether balancing of accounts included preparing summary accounts. Schmalenbach, in *Dynamic Accounting*, concentrates on *Summa* Chapter 32, which deals with the "sum of sums" as a final proof of closing a ledger whose balances are transferred to another ledger. For this purpose summary accounts are, of course, not required. A more useful reference is to *Summa* Chapter 34, where Pacioli says: "There are certain accounts which one may not wish to transfer, such as expenses and income. These accounts should therefore be closed to a profit and loss account." It is clear that here Pacioli had the preparation of summary accounts in mind.

Although Pacioli recognised yearly balancing of accounts, it is not certain that he appreciated the concept of periodic income and expense. There is no treatment of the problems of accruals and prepayments in the *Summa*, and this could be due to Pacioli's not recognising the importance of this procedure, or it might be that he did not think it practical. In the *Summa*, transactions are recorded on the basis of cash receipts and payments for the period, even though income and expenditure accounting was a known fifteenth-century practice.

Pacioli certainly recognised the concept of consistency when he wrote: "Woe to anyone who has anything to do with people who desire to keep the books in their own way, and are always persuading you to believe that their way is better than that of any of the others and for such reasons they sometimes mix up the accounts of the said officers in such a manner that they do not correspond in any way." The concept is also apparent in Pacioli's insistence that from the journal onwards the books should be written by one person, to ensure consistent treatment of detail.

It is apparent from the general nature of the text that Pacioli recognised the accounting entity, although he envisaged it in a way different from modern practice. If the business was conducted in the home, all personal property was included in the inventory, and the expenses of the home were included in the accounts for the year. If part of the operations of the organisation were conducted by an employee at a different address, agency accounting was used. Goods sent to the manager of the outside branch were debited to the manager's personal account, and any payments received by him and transmitted to the owner of the goods were credited. Where several different types of business were carried out by the same person at one address, only one accounting entity would be recognised. Pacioli's accounting entity was physical in concept—a home, a person or a counting house.

It could well be that, reflecting as it did the practice of Venetian merchants, Pacioli's book was somewhat behind the times as compared with current practice in other Italian cities. Venice was a centre of trade, mainly with the Middle East, where conditions were always uncertain. This could account for the advocacy of cash accounting, and for the failure to deal adequately with financial reporting, or at all with auditing or costing; these were not subjects of concern to merchants mainly engaged in trading by foreign ventures. By comparison, Florence was a considerable manufacturing centre and had important financial institutions, besides being engaged in world trade. The more advanced accounting methods used there, and elsewhere, are likely to have been the product of more complex, and more enduring business organisations than were common in Venice.

The "Italian Method"

Few examples of accounting records created in the years immediately following 1500 are now available, but it seems not unlikely that the example of the Italian merchants, aided by the publication of Pacioli's *Summa*, spread double-entry methods across Europe. Probably it was more because of the influence of Italian merchants, who were using the system, than Pacioli's first description of it, that double-entry became generally known as the "Italian Method".

Although in the 30 years following Pacioli's treatise no known further works on the subject were published, the following 70 years saw the appearance of many books, in several languages, all based more or less on the *Summa*. As Hatfield says:[1] "It is nearly true to say that for a hundred years the texts appearing in England, France, Germany, Italy and the Low Countries were, at the best, revisions of Pacioli, at the worst, servile transcriptions without even the courtesy of referring to the original author."

Domenico Manzoni's *Quaderno doppio col suo giornale secondo il costume di Venetio*, which ran to six editions between 1540 and 1574, is typical. It is of a more practical nature than Pacioli's text, including illustrations of the working of an effective set of double-entry books, yet in many parts Manzoni followed Pacioli word for word.

The first English publication on the subject was Hugh Oldcastle's *Profitable Treatyce* which appeared in 1543,[2] and this

[1] An Historical Defence of Book-keeping, p.4 in Baxter (Ed.), *Studies in Accounting*, London, 1950.

[2] The titles of the early texts have been abbreviated. For instance, Oldcastle's book was called *A Profitable Treatyce called the Instrument or Boke to learne to knowe the good order of the keepyng of the famous reconyge called in Latyn, Dare and Habere, and in Englyshe, Debitor and Creditor.*

seems to have been a fairly close copy of Pacioli. Unfortunately, no known copy of the book now exists, but the essence of it is contained in John Mellis's *The Briefe Instruction*, published in 1588. Mellis says "I am but the renewer of an ancient old copie printed here in London . . . then collected and published, made and set forth by one Hugh Oldcastle."

An important early book was Ympyn's *Notable and Excellent Woorke* which was published simultaneously in French and Dutch in 1543, an English translation becoming available in 1547. It seems certain that, in the sixteenth and seventeenth centuries, double-entry methods were both more commonly and more effectively used on the Continent, and particularly in Holland, than in England. John Waddington, who published his *Breffe Instruction* in 1567, and Richard Dafforne, who wrote *The Merchant's Mirrour* in 1635, both had experience of Dutch commercial practice, and Dafforne testified to the use of more advanced methods in Holland than in England. Dafforne's book, which was a competent expression of accounting method, was probably the first English work to be widely read. It ran to several editions, and stimulated interest in the subject in England to a considerable extent.

Pacioli had a substantial influence on these early writers. Some improvements were suggested—for instance, by James Peel who, in his book *Pathway to Perfectness* (1569), advocated the use of several waste books, each special to a particular class of transactions, and the abolition of the journal; and somewhat later, in 1789, Benjamin Booth suggested the use of the waste book to summarise entries before posting to the ledger. No doubt the several writers relied to some extent on each other. Thus Mellis borrowed ideas from both Waddington and Peel, whilst Peel was influenced by Manzoni, who, in turn, depended largely on Pacioli. It is interesting to compare Mellis's description of the trial balance with Pacioli's. Mellis wrote:

"The ballance of your booke is to be understoode, a leafe of paper disposed and made in length and crossed in the middes, in such wise that it have two faces in plaine sighte, uppon which leafe on the right side, yee shal copy al the Creditors, with their restes according. That don, beholde if that the summe of the Debitor, be as much as the summe of the Creditor, and yf the summes of money, of Debitor and Creditor bee alike, then is your ballance well, and appeareth evidently, that your bookes have been orderly kept and governed."

Pacioli's words were:

"The balance of the ledger is understood to be a sheet of paper creased lengthwise, on the right-hand side of which are copied the credits of the ledger and on the left-hand side the debits, and check if the sum of the debits is the same as that of the credits and if so the ledger is correct."

Some later writers challenged the validity of Pacioli's method. In 1796 Edward Jones published a book which decried the Italian system, in somewhat intemperate terms, as being misleading and prone to error, and suggested a system based on single entry. Jones's book, which was published in the United States in 1797 and translated into several foreign languages, was the first English work to acquire an international reputation. This was unfortunate since, after some initial success, his ideas failed to gain general acceptance.

It is difficult to say to what extent the development of accounting was influenced by the early writers. Double-entry pre-dated Pacioli by more than a century, and his book was not an exposition of the best practice of his day. Subsequent writers added little to the original text of the *Summa*. Yet development there must have been. Even as double-entry had its origins in the counting houses of the Italian merchants, the later growth of trade throughout Europe must have produced refinements in the system as it was used in practice. Perhaps the most one can say for the early writers is that they spread abroad the basic ideas of accounting, ideas around which businessmen could design recording systems suited to their needs. But to say that is to say a good deal. The information disseminated by Pacioli and his successors provided the basis on which practitioners could build the methods of modern financial recording and reporting. No doubt the "Italian method" would have spread abroad through the international connections of trading concerns but, without the aid of the early texts, development would certainly have been slower.

Discussion Topics

1. Chapter 1 might be described as a matter of purely historic interest. Does it, as such, merit the attention of students of modern accountancy?

2. "Accounting by double-entry has substantial advantages over the unco-ordinated recording methods used earlier." What are these advantages?

3. Though double-entry might have been the invention of some scholar or businessman, it is more likely that it developed gradually over a period of time, as the work of the counting houses became more complex through the diversification of trade and the growth of manufacturing. By what steps might accounting records have changed from unrelated inventories to a co-ordinated double-entry system?

4. How important to the development of accounting was the work of Luca Pacioli?

5. Pacioli's *Summa* did not contain a comprehensive treatment of the known accounting practices of his time. Why might this have been?

6. Might the "sum of sums" referred to in *Summa* Chapter 32 be described, in modern terminology, as a "trial balance"?

CHAPTER 2

The Industrial Revolution: Demand and Response

PACIOLI and subsequent early writers concerned themselves solely with the accounts of merchants and traders, and this is not surprising. Though there were exceptions, medieval manufacturing, largely organised on the guild system, was a matter of small-scale operation, a master and up to half a dozen employees constituting the business. In such circumstances, accounts showing internal flows of value would hardly be necessary, and, in any case, several early writers expressed the belief that the double-entry system was not capable of application to manufacturing operations. In 1697, however, John Collins published his *Perfect Method of Merchants Accounts*, which contained an illustration of a set of dyers' accounts, and this was probably the first book in English to demonstrate that it was possible to apply double-entry to industrial as well as to commercial record keeping.

Developments which followed the land enclosure movements raised some new accounting problems. Capitalist manufacturers, who gave out materials to be worked up by artisans in their own homes, required stock accounts and records of materials issued to, and returned by, outworkers, and amounts earned by them. Two books dealing with the accountability of outworkers were James Doodson's *The Accountant or the Method of Book-keeping* (1750) and Wardlaugh Thompson's *The Accomptant's Oracle* (1777), which described effective systems of recording for, respectively, shoemaking and hosiery manufacture. Associated with the same movement, Roger North's book *The Gentleman Accomptant*, which was published in 1714, gave attention to pastoral accounting, advocating separate accounts for "husbandry", "grazing and dairy" and "flocks", so that the profit

15

or loss on each might be shown. An interesting book was Robert Hamilton's *Introduction to Merchandise*, which was published in 1788. Besides dealing with pastoral accounting, and suggesting separate accounts for each field so that the costs and revenues from various crops in different years might be ascertained, he demonstrated an elementary form of industrial cost analysis, including records of materials purchased and consumed, a wages book, expense accounts, and accounts to show the results of each process of production or aspect of trade. It seems, however, that Hamilton's writing was well in advance of the general commercial practice of his time. He was a political economist and mathematician, and was Professor of Philosophy at the Marischal College in Aberdeen.

The Factory System

Growth in the size of the typical manufacturing unit, which was slow until the middle of the eighteenth century, accelerated under the impetus of the discovery of new, mechanical methods of manufacture and improved means of transportation. The replacement of outworking by factory working, and the migration into the factory centres of much of the previously rural population presented many and novel problems of production control for the early factory capitalists. The treatment of the capital cost and depreciation of buildings and machinery, growing quickly in size and value, the control of stocks of raw materials and finished goods and of work in progress, estimating and tendering for contracts, price fixing and the control of large labour forces were all industrial demands to which there must have been an accounting response. No doubt industrialists were resolving accounting problems within their own businesses but, following Hamilton's book, very little was written on the subject in England for nearly a century. This is surprising. It might have been expected that the country which first experienced the Industrial Revolution would have led the way in factory accounting literature. As R. S. Edwards says:

"It is difficult to account for the absence of works on industrial accountancy in the next eighty or ninety years [after 1788]. Books on commercial accounting were turned out by the dozen, but with one or two slight exceptions writers on accountancy neglected the problems of the industrial community at a time when the latter was being revolutionised by power, the factory system, and the growth of communications."[1]

As late as 1869 a leading article in *The Engineer* deplored the inaccuracies of engineers' estimates, and said that one "right within twenty per cent of the actual cost is, however, regarded as a very good estimate, and one reflecting much credit on the engineer and all concerned. . . . There is no good treatise on the subject".

French writers seem to have found the subject more rewarding. A book published in Paris in 1817 described, with illustrations from three quite different kinds of business, an accounting system with separate, but reconcilable financial and costing records, and stores accounts (though dealing with quantities only), and demonstrated the inclusion of items such as depreciation, rent and interest in reported costs. Another French book, which appeared 10 years later, dealt effectively with process costing, the depreciation and maintenance of buildings and machinery, and the problem of charging to production materials bought at varying prices. Furthermore, this book included an explanation of perpetual inventory recording.

After 1870 there was a revival of interest in industrial accounting among English writers. A significant contribution was Garke and Fells' *Factory Accounts*, which was published in 1887, and which demonstrated the integration of cost and financial records, suggesting a Prime Cost Ledger, with an account for each job done in the works, and overhead accounts in which costs not allocable to jobs could be collected for subsequent redistribution on the basis of direct labour or machine hours worked. G. P.

[1] *Accountant*, London, 1937, vol. XCVII, p.254. In a series of articles in this volume Edwards deals comprehensively with the development of cost accounts, and gives illustrations of accounting forms taken from early records.

Norton was another writer whose work had an important impact over a long period of time. As early as 1891 Norton was pointing out the need for departmental costs in an article in the *Accountant,* and in his book *Cost Accounting and Cost Control* (1931) he advocated the use of standard costs rather than outside prices as the test of efficient operation.

The renaissance in cost accounting literature can be attributed directly to the increasing problems confronting manufacturers in the more competitive conditions of trade of the early twentieth century. With the development of industrial power in the United States of America the day had passed when British manufacturers had unrestricted access to world markets for their output, and competitive pricing requires effective means of identification of, and control over, costs of production. A major problem was to determine appropriate means of attaching overheads to production, and the common method of a percentage on wages was being attacked as early as 1878 by Thomas Battersby and later, in 1891, by Sir John Mann. The major contribution to the debate was, however, made by Alexander Hamilton Church. Church was an English electrical engineer, who migrated to the United States around 1900. He conceived the idea of splitting down the factory into "production centres", subdivisions of the total production process among which overhead costs could first be divided for subsequent allocation to output on the basis of machine hour rates. Mass production and the ideas of scientific management, which saw rapid development in America in the first decade of the twentieth century, required effective factory accounting, and the name of Alexander Hamilton Church is linked with those of the other pioneers, Gannt, Nicholson and Winslow Taylor.

Another question of moment was the distinction between fixed and variable costs, i.e. costs which remain constant irrespective of the level of output, and costs which vary as production expands or contracts. This has obvious implications when changes in the level of output are contemplated. Garke and Fells, in their early book, had the genesis of the idea when they suggested that: "There is no advantage in distributing these items over the various transactions. They do not vary proportionately with the volume of business. . . . The principals of a business can always judge what percentage of gross profits upon cost is necessary to cover fixed establishment charges and interest on capital." [1] By 1903, however, Henry Hess, in an article in the *Engineering Magazine* was able to explain the relationship between fixed and variable costs and output to the stage at which it could be demonstrated on a chart, along with total receipts for each level of output, the "modern" concept of the break-even chart.

Many examples of accounting response to industrial demand after 1900 could be given. Harrington Emerson was writing advanced work on standard costs from 1908, the use of budgets for controlling actual expenditure was described by S. H. Bunnell in 1911, and uniform costing had its origins, mainly in the United States, around the turn of the century. It is not a process that has ceased, nor is likely to do so. Business conditions are never static, and yesterday's procedures are unlikely to be able adequately to satisfy modern demands. Industrial accounting will remain relevant only for so long as it continues to meet each new challenge with an immediate response, and there is no lack of challenge. The development of new data processing, storage, and data retrieval equipment has made available to industrialists quantities and qualities of information which are having effects not only on the decision making process, but on the whole structure of management in industry. The interpretation and use of information about production, marketing and finance has replaced the recording function as the chief occupation of management accountants, and in maximising the utility of novel, more complex, and more pertinent information systems in the continuing, and growing Industrial Revolution lies the exciting future of industrial accounting.

Limited Liability

The Industrial Revolution has not been solely a technical revolution. The new machinery, the factories required to house

[1] Garke and Fells, *Factory Accounts*, 1st edn., p.74. London, 1887

it, the labour forces needed to operate it, and the increased inventories of all sorts, from raw materials to finished goods, called forth by longer and more complex production cycles, have all demanded greatly increased financial resources. If advantage was to be taken of the new technology it was essential that means of generating industrial capital be devised.

Early attempts to finance factory development naturally took the form of partnerships. Manufacturers who had been working on their own, on a limited scale, joined together to pool both their expertise and their resources, but the pace of development was too fast for arrangements of this kind to provide adequate capital in the long period. Partnership has, in addition, other disadvantages. Partners die, or withdraw from the association, or prove to have resources inadequate to sustain the firm through periods of adverse trading conditions. Furthermore, it is a general principle of partnership that each partner has the right to a share in the management of the firm, and that a man is wealthy is no guarantee that he is well endowed with managerial talent.

The joint stock company was not a new idea in Britain in the nineteenth century. From the seventeenth century companies such as the East India Company and the Hudson Bay Company had been operating, with the liability of their members for company debts subject to limitations defined in their charters of incorporation, but such companies were exceptional. They were created by Royal Charter, usually with the object of conducting trade with some distant territory, and it was not to be until long after the charter companies had led the way that the devices of separate corporate personality and limited liability for shareholders were to be applied generally to production and trade.

By 1844 partnership enterprise had clearly become inadequate as a means of organising industrial activity. A committee of the British Parliament, reporting in that year, pointed out that there were serious disadvantages in large joint-stock partnerships, in particular, because not all partners took part in management, there was ample scope for the falsification of unaudited accounts. The Joint-Stock Companies Act, 1844, was the first statute to make it possible to form a company by the comparatively simple method of registration with the Registrar of Joint-Stock Companies. Though the Act made no provision for limitation of the liability of shareholders in the new joint-stock companies, it did provide some measure of protection for shareholders by requiring that books of account be kept, and periodically balanced, that a "full and fair" balance sheet be presented to the shareholders at each annual meeting, and that auditors be appointed, charged with the duty of reporting on the balance sheets presented to the shareholders. The Act required that a copy of the audited balance sheet presented to the shareholders be filed with the Registrar of Joint-Stock Companies.

The principle of limited liability for shareholders in joint stock companies was first introduced by British Acts of Parliament in 1855 and 1856, but these Acts removed the compulsory accounting and auditing provisions which had been introduced in 1844. The reasons seem to have been that matters of account are confidential, and for private debate between directors and shareholders only, and that it had proved difficult to frame a compulsory scheme of financial reporting which would adequately protect shareholder interests. A model form of balance sheet was, however, appended to the 1856 Act, and the model articles of association also provided included sections on accounting and auditing matters. Such remained the situation in Britain until the Companies Act of 1900 reintroduced an obligatory audit for registered companies. Since that date successive measures have increased the powers of auditors, have specified the qualifications they must have before appointment, and have required progressively more information to be included in reports made to shareholders and filed with the Registrar of Companies.

Developments in the United States followed a somewhat different pattern. Corporation legislation was first introduced in Connecticut in 1837, and other states soon followed suit, but there were substantial differences in provisions concerning both audit and disclosure of information in the Acts of the several states, and because of weaknesses in the statutes of some states, the New York Stock Exchange began to make agreements with companies whose shares were traded on the exchange concerning the observance of certain uniform accounting principles, and providing for the disclosure of adequate information in published company reports.

Limited company enterprise has developed not only in England and America, but also in Europe and Australasia as the normal form of large-scale industrial organisation. Its advantages are several. In the first instance it enables many investors to participate in industrial activity without incurring the legal liabilities of partnership. In simple terms the principle of limited liability means that the purchaser of a share is under no obligation to contribute to the liabilities of the company beyond a fixed sum for each share he has bought. In effect, a limited liability company is a separate legal person from its shareholders, and the creditors of the company can look only to the assets of the company itself for satisfaction of their debts. The diminished risk in investment which company development provided has resulted in the collection of very large sums of money for industrial and commercial purposes. Though considerable investment had earlier taken place in statutory companies, particularly in the field of transportation—railways and canals—it seems impossible that the impetus of the Industrial Revolution could have been maintained if it had not been for the device of the limited liability company in bringing the savings of many investors, large and small, to productive use in capitalising industrial enterprise.

A second advantage of joint-stock incorporation is that it facilitates the divorce of the management of businesses from the ownership of capital. It by no means follows that those most able to finance an industrial concern are well equipped to manage it. Neither does it follow that the most efficient managers will have enough money to finance the concern they are managing. In joint-stock companies, boards of directors are elected by the shareholders, each shareholder having, as a rule, one vote for each share he holds. It is not infrequently the case that the owners of a company are many shareholders, with little, if any, technical knowledge of the company's operations, whilst management is in the hands of a small number of experts in the company's business. Though not infrequently shareholders fail to exercise their voting rights at the election of directors, and in consequence the process of such election is not as democratic as it might be, the development of joint-stock company enterprise has contributed largely to the growth of professional, and efficient, industrial management.

The Accountancy Profession

Speculation exists as to the date when accountants first began public practice. As custodians of titles to property and in giving effect to transfers of property under wills and settlements, lawyers provided an early accounting service in a limited area for some of their clients.

Following the confiscation of the estates of certain Scottish lairds after the 1745 rising, it appears probable that some agents accepted responsibility for rendering accounts of confiscated estates on a professional basis. Others, retained to protect the interests of creditors by accepting assignments of bankrupts' property, to realise these properties and distribute the proceeds amongst the creditors, were probably drawn from commercial pursuits. Such was the demand for services of this kind that occasional assignments became permanent occupations.

By the beginning of the nineteenth century accountants were engaging in private practice in many cities, but particularly in Scotland. Their interests were wide. One James McClelland published a circular in 1824, when he commenced business, announcing that he was willing to undertake the following work: [1]

"Factor and trustee of sequestrated estates.
Trustee or factor for trustees of creditors acting under trust deeds.
Factor for trustees acting for the heirs of persons deceased.

[1] Brown, *History of Accounting and Accountants,* Edinburgh, 1905.

Factor for gentlemen residing in the country for the management of heritable or other property.

Agent for houses in England and Scotland connected with bankruptcies in Glasgow.

The winding up of dissolved partnership concerns and the adjusting of partners' accounts.

The keeping and balancing of all account-books belonging to merchants, manufacturers, shopkeepers, etc.

The examining and adjusting of all disputed accounts and account-books.

The making up of statements, reports, and memorials on account-books or disputed accounts and claims for the purpose of laying before arbiters, courts, or counsel.

And all other departments of the accountant business."

The main impetus for the growth of professional practice in accountancy, however, was the development of limited company enterprise. The earliest Companies Acts contained a provision requiring accounts to be presented to shareholders at specific intervals. Subsequent Acts have increased and specified the amount of information which must be supplied, and as the divorce of ownership and management has developed, provisions relating to the audit of company accounts have become an essential feature of company legislation. The professional accountant, acting as auditor, is the representative of the shareholders, often charged with the duty of reporting, on their behalf, that the accounts presented by the directors show a true and fair view of the activities of the company.

Nor was auditing the only field of employment opened for accountants by limited company legislation. Accountants were active in advising on the formation of companies, their reconstruction, amalgamation, subdivision and winding-up, and were representing shareholders, debenture holders and creditors, besides acting in many ways for companies themselves. It may well be said that the practising accountant has become the limited company's family doctor. He acts as midwife at its birth, corrects its childhood ailments, gives it an annual check-up, is present at any weddings, supervises the birth of children, signs the death certificate, and, as often as not, deals with the deceased's estate!

The accountancy profession thus developed in two separate, though related, ways. Accountants in public practice drew their business from the increasing complexity of company finance, from governmental action, particularly in the field of taxation, and from the widening basis of industrial investment. In industry, accountants were concerned with the control of increasing quantities of capital equipment and other productive factors, and with the formation of management decisions. It can be argued that the work done by the two groups is so dissimilar as to justify their division into two professions, but both groups base their practice of accountancy on the same principles, they have a common history, and the transfer of accountants from one sector of the profession to the other is by no means uncommon.

Professional Organisation

The professional organisation of accountancy began among accountants in public practice. Though the number of accountants in practice at the beginning of the nineteenth century was small, it quickly increased. There seem to have been 24 accountants in practice in London in 1811, 107 in 1840, 264 in 1850 and 467 in 1870. In Manchester there were 14 in 1815, 52 in 1840 and 159 in 1871,[1] and similar rates of growth were to be found in other cities in the United Kingdom.

The earliest professional organisations were formed in Scotland. Royal charters were granted to societies of accountants in Edinburgh and Glasgow in 1854, and in Aberdeen in 1867.[2] In England and Wales, incorporated societies of accountants which had been formed in Liverpool and London in 1870, in Manchester in 1873 and in Sheffield in 1874 amalgamated to form the Institute of Chartered Accountants in England and Wales in 1880.

[1] Brown, *History of Accounting and Accountants,* Edinburgh, 1905.
[2] These have subsequently amalgamated to constitute the Institute of Chartered Accountants of Scotland.

The profession in the United States had a later beginning. In 1905 Richard Brown wrote: "There is one gentleman still living, however, who commenced business in Boston in 1847; but for a year or two he was the sole representative of the profession in that city, and it was many years before it was regarded with much favour." Not until 1887 was the American Association of Public Accountants formed and at its meeting in 1889 its membership was only 32. In 1896, however, an Act was passed in the State of New York to regulate the profession of public accountant. It provided for suitably qualified persons to be registered as public accountants, to have the title Certified Public Accountant, and to use the abbreviation C.P.A. after their names. The New York Act provided an example which was copied in the other states of the union in succeeding years. American C.P.A.'s sit a common examination set by the American Institute of Certified Public Accountants, but are issued with their certificates of practice by the states in which they are domiciled. The states vary in their requirements with regard to general education and professional experience. Some accept only experience in public accountancy as a condition of admission to qualified status, but others accept experience in industry and commerce, and some states require very little experience of any kind.

Organisation of the accountancy profession in Canada began with the incorporation of the Association of Accountants in Montreal in 1880, to be followed in 1883 by the Institute of Chartered Accountants in Ontario. Similar developments in other Canadian provinces followed, and the modern Canadian Institute of Chartered Accountants is a federation of ten provincial institutes, membership of the national body following automatically upon admission to membership of any one of the provincial institutes. As in the United States, there is a uniform qualifying examination throughout the country, but other requirements and conditions before admission to the Institute vary from province to province. In most provinces, training in public accountancy is a prerequisite to admission, but in some, industrial or commercial experience is recognised.

The Institute of Accountants in South Australia was formed in 1889, and similar organisations in other Australian states appeared before the end of the century, and in New Zealand the Incorporated Institute of Accountants was founded in 1894. These pioneer Australasian bodies have led to the formation of national Institutes or Societies of Chartered Accountants.

Demand and Response

Since the beginning of the Industrial Revolution, economic development in Europe and America, and later in Australasia, has been continuous, though there have been periods of relative stagnation, particularly in the 1930's, and disastrous experiences such as the two World Wars. The volume and diversity of production, the size of business organisations and the problems of finance have all increased apace. Upon this swelling tide of economic expansion the accountancy profession has been borne forth. In industry and commerce, in banking, insurance and foreign trade, in the service of governments and universities besides in public practice, accountants are playing an invaluable part in the direction of business and government.

Double-entry was created in response to the challenge of fifteenth-century commercial enterprise. The accountancy profession grew out of the economic demands of the Industrial Revolution. The greater the complexity of the structure of production and exchange, the more important it is that financial information and advice should be given with competence and honesty. It is for this purpose that the accountancy profession of today exists, and upon its ability to respond to the demands of the future will its continued progress depend.

Discussion Topics

1. Why did Pacioli and the other early writers concern themselves solely with the accounts of merchants and traders?.

2. Must accounting *always* be a response to some economic or social development? Does not Robert Hamilton's work suggest that accounting

might generate economic or social change by providing information not previously available?

3. What novel problems of production control must the beginning of the factory system have created?

4. The development of cost accounting has been said to have been mainly the product of two circumstances; increasing competition in international trade as the Industrial Revolution spread to the United States, Germany and other countries, and the economic depressions of the inter-war period. What kinds of impact might these events have had on industrial accounting?

5. Might the Industrial Revolution be said to have been not only a technical, but also a financial revolution?

6. What are the advantages and disadvantages of the incorporation of a business as a limited liability company? It has been said that accountants "act as midwives at the birth of companies", but could it not also be said that the accountancy profession is the offspring of the limited liability movement?

PART II **THEORY**

CHAPTER 3

A Conceptual Framework

THE production and exchange of goods and services are the basic economic activities of society, and accounting is a reflection of those activities, a practical matter of recording and analysing manufacturing and trading information so that significant totals of gain or loss and net worth might be presented. It has been defined by the American Institute of Certified Public Accountants in the following terms: [1]

"Accounting is the art of recording, classifying, and summarising in a significant manner and in terms of money, transactions and events which are, in part at least, of a financial character, and interpreting the results thereof."

The word "significant" in the definition means significant to the recipient of the reports, pertinent to his business objectives and in accord with the economic, legal and political conditions of society at the time of the report. There is, in consequence, always a conceptual frame, stated or unstated, within which accounting works. The accounts of the Renaissance merchants and manufacturers were far removed from the uncorrelated inventories of earlier times; their business affairs had developed to a stage where the comprehensive recording of the transactions of defined units of account was necessary, where the desirability of dividing the lives of continuing businesses into accounting periods was recognised, and where it was appreciated that cash-flow figures could be adjusted for accrued and prepaid income and expenditure, so that more meaningful measures of net income might be made. They knew no stated theory of accounting, yet the unstated assumptions underlying their accounts constituted a conceptual

[1] *Accounting Terminology Bulletin No.* 1, A.I.C.P.A., 1953.

31

framework, drawn from the contemporary business environment, within which their accounts were drawn.

Because accounting seeks to represent the financial transactions of a continually changing economy, neither practice nor theory is static. The continuing process of the industrial revolution, effecting progressive development of the economic, social, legal and political organisation of society, has necessitated changes in the conceptual framework of accounting, and no doubt will continue to do so, and it is because there have been changes, because the conditions of production and exchange have become so complex, that the demand for a stated theory of accounting has arisen. Accounting is not solely a matter of recording and classifying. It involves summarisation and interpretation, discretionary tasks requiring the exercise of judgement, and the conceptual frame as it has now developed seeks to limit the discretionary area, and to provide guidance where the exercise of judgement is necessary.

An alternative way of looking at accounting is to regard it as a process whereby the mass of data pertinent to an economic activity is reduced to a single summary document or series of documents on the basis of which past performance and present position might be gauged, and as a guide to future policy. As the volume of information relevant to business activity has become greater, and more complex, the task of providing aggregate statements which reflect, and do not distort the underlying reality has become progressively harder. It is probably true to say that, in modern commercial conditions, it would not be possible for any short series of documents to represent with accuracy the financial progress and present position of an economic unit of any magnitude, and that the best that can be done by accounting theory is to specify a code of procedures which, if they do not eliminate distortions, at least tend to codify practice in those areas where distortion is likeliest to occur.

Accounting theory thus has its basis in practical experience of changing economic and social circumstances. Variously described as doctrines, conventions, postulates, etc., by different writers, the concepts which collectively constitute the framework of accounting are the product of reasoning about the most appropriate ways to record transactions and interpret totals in actual business situations, as they present themselves in the context of modern economic and social conditions.

The Boundaries of Accountability

The first group of propositions in accounting theory is concerned with the limits on accountability. It is not possible just "to account", there must be something to account *for*, and a *period of time* during which the accounted transactions took place. A part of the conceptual framework consists of the definition of these physical, and temporal, boundaries on accounting.

The Accounting Entity

The concept of the accounting entity stems from the idea that there is a boundary around the area of economic activity with which each set of accounting records is concerned, and to which each series of financial reports is relevant. The entity can be conceived in physical terms as a group of assets devoted to the pursuit of a specified economic objective or group of objectives, together with the co-extensive claims on those assets of proprietors, investors and creditors.

The simplest situation is where the whole of a business, whether owned by one person, or a partnership, or a public company, constitutes the entity. All the transactions of the firm pass through a single accounting system and are summarised in one income statement and balance sheet, but it does not necessarily follow that an accounting entity will be coincident with any *legal* entity. Thus, as a matter of convenience, a sole trader might choose to regard his business operations as a separate accounting entity, an area of economic activity separate from his personal estate, requiring separate records and financial reports, but such an entity is not legally separate from its owner. In the event of the assets of the entity being inadequate to satisfy the demands of its creditors, recourse could be made to the reality behind the entity—the real and legal person of the owner himself. The same is true of a partnership. Even though the separate existence of the accounting entity is clearly apparent in that it constitutes a collection of assets contributed by a number of persons trading in common, in the event of the failure of the business the partners would be jointly and severally liable for its debts and obligations.

A public company constitutes a legal entity, but even here the legal and accounting entities sometimes fail to coincide. Many businesses, especially those active in diverse fields or in different countries, divide their assets and liabilities and business transactions into separate operating units, each of which might constitute an accounting entity in the sense that they are separate areas of economic activity, requiring separate accounting records and financial reports. Though it is material to the legal entity it is not material to the accounting entity whether a business is organised as a holding company with subsidiaries or as a unitary company with departments and branches. The essence of the accounting entity is that it is a group of assets and business operations *considered by the asset owners and the transaction directors to be distinct and separate from any other assets and operations.* The physical dimensions of the unit of account—the entity—are determined by those for whom the records will be kept, and to whom the reports will be presented and, particularly where there is no coincidence between the accounting and some legal entity, it is important that the boundaries of account should be clearly drawn, that the relationships between separate entities within a single business be specified, and that the degree of separation of the entity from the personal estates of proprietors be understood.

The Period of Account

Besides the physical boundary on the accounting process expressed in the concept of the accounting entity, there is a boundary of time. An income statement is concerned not only with what profit or loss has resulted from the employment of the assets of an entity but also with the period of time taken to achieve those results, and a balance sheet does more than tabulate the assets and liabilities of an entity, it tabulates them as they were at a point in time.

The accounting period was not a problem which troubled the early merchant venturers greatly. Accounts were opened for each trading venture and were closed on its completion, by which time all the costs and revenue associated with the venture would be known, and the profit or loss could be determined with accuracy. Such is sometimes the case today—partnerships are on occasions formed for limited periods and purposes, but most modern businesses continue indefinitely, and there are both legal and managerial reasons for the preparation of periodic income statements and balance sheets.

The two major legal requirements for periodic reporting stem from the development of limited liability company enterprise and the growth in importance of taxation. The primary motive for investment in a limited company is the expectation of dividends, and the determination of whether or not there are surpluses available for distribution as dividend depends on periodic accounting calculations. Furthermore, company legislation has, from the beginning, required that directors prepare periodic accounts of their stewardship for presentation to the shareholders. Income tax laws have had like effect: the imposition of the tax would not be possible in the absence of periodic calculations of income, but their impact has been broader than that of the company legislation. Not only limited companies but also partnerships and individuals must pay income tax, with the result that periodic reporting of income has become required of all types of business enterprise.

Statutory reporting periods are almost always calendar years; companies are required to file annual reports, and income taxes are levied on reported annual incomes but, these legal requirements apart, there is nothing sacrosanct about the calendar year as the accounting period of an entity. Even as the physical boundaries which constitute the entity are determined by its owners and directors, so is the accounting period *used for their own purposes* a matter for their discretion. It is unlikely that a year would be the most suitable period of account for internal management purposes in the dynamic conditions of modern business; some shorter period, a quarter, month, or week might be considered necessary for the adequate control and direction of the resources of a business. Nor is it essential that periods of account should be equal in length. Special factors such as seasonal trends in production or sales, or variable lengths of production cycles (e.g. in the building industry), might suggest that accounting periods of varying lengths would be more appropriate to managerial needs in some cases.

The central position of company reporting and tax calculation in accounting practice has led to the emphasis on the year as the period of account. The great majority of accounting reports, however, are prepared not to satisfy legal requirements but to inform executives on the progress and position of their enterprises, and even as there is no *necessary* coincidence between a legal and an accounting entity, there is no *necessary* coincidence between statutory and managerial accounting periods.

Measurement Assumptions

The second part of the conceptual framework of accounting consists of two assumptions on the basis of which the recording process is founded.

Monetary Measurement

The definition with which this chapter began contains the words "in terms of money" and, though entities might keep records of inventories and statistics of production or sales in other units, monetary recording is an essential of accounting. An account is such only if it expresses transactions in terms of money.

The main advantage of monetary recording is that money can be used as a common measure for diverse types of income and expenditure, assets and liabilities. Thus factory statistics might show the quantities of material, the amount of factory space and the number of labour hours required to achieve a given output, but these can only sensibly be aggregated into a product cost in money terms. Similarly a factory might contain quantities of machinery, of a variety of types, and it might be useful to have an inventory, but for most practical purposes it would be more useful to know the value of the several classes of assets, and the total value in so many dollars, pounds or yen.

Besides being the common denominator in terms of which the aggregate of flows of value within the firm can be expressed, money is the external medium of exchange. By the expenditure of money, factors of production are obtained, output is sold for money, and it is the expectation of dividends in money that induces most investors to subscribe the monetary capital of industry. Accounting is concerned with the measurement of income, and of value, and such measurements are normally made in money terms. Whatever else money might be the root of, it is certainly the root of accounting.

The use of money as the recording unit in accounting is in accord with commercial practice in developed economies, and has the advantage of being the only common measure of the value of the many and very diverse commodities and services employed in the mechanisms of production and exchange, but it has disadvantages. In the first instance, at the point of exchange, when sales or purchases are made, money received or paid is a fair expression of value given or obtained, but money is not a stable unit of measurement, its purchasing power is subject to continual change, and the further in time from the point of exchange an asset is held or a liability sustained, the less effective as a measure of value is the original exchange price. It would be possible to adjust historic costs so that they more accurately represented current values, but to do so would introduce substantial elements of subjective judgement into accounting computations, and the present consensus of opinion is that *the monetary unit used in accounting is exchange price, irrespective of the point in time when the exchange took place.* [1]

Further limitations of monetary accounting should be recognised. Money measurements of income, revenue, expense, assets and liabilities are not the whole story about any business. Many industrial and commercial factors are incapable of expression in money, or for that matter in any quantitative terms. Accounting reveals the cost of production but does not describe the quality of the product. It reveals the expense of administration but makes no comment on the efficiency of management. It assigns values to inventories, but says nothing about their appropriateness to the future objectives of the firm or the condition of the market. Accounting has much to say about the conduct of business affairs, but it would be a mistake to assume that all the factors relevant to almost any business situation can be expressed in terms of money.

Continuity of Activity

Some businesses have short and known life periods, and it is sometimes the case that the ending of an established business can be predicted—when, for instance, proceedings in bankruptcy or for liquidation of a company have been instituted. Where this is so it is a matter of common business prudence that assets and liabilities should be valued, and revenue and expense measured having regard to the known circumstances of the situation. More commonly, however, businesses, and particularly company enterprises, have indefinite lives; there is no foreseeable end to their operations when transactions are recorded and when financial reports are presented. It is therefore common accounting practice to *regard an entity as remaining in operation indefi-*

[1] "It [value in exchange] does *not* include 'subjective values' or 'intrinsic values' which rest on people's tastes and hopes. Subjective values of this type are undoubtedly useful in welfare economics; they have no place, however, in accounting." Maurice Moonitz, *The Basic Postulates of Accounting,* A.I.C.P.A. Research Study No. 1, 1961, at p.19.

nitely in the absence of evidence to the contrary. This does not mean that accountants assume that entities *will* have indefinite lives but only that if there is no present intention to terminate the life of an entity, there is no reason to adopt the special asset valuation and income measurement techniques appropriate to the circumstances of business cessation.

The main impact on accounting records and reports of this assumption is the effect it has on the values assigned to various classes of business assets. Thus accounts receivable are valued at the sum which it is estimated will eventually be collected in cash, usually the gross figure less a provision for doubtful debts, and not at their value if they had tò be disposed of immediately (e.g. to a debt-collecting agency). Similarly, inventories of raw materials and partly finished goods are valued in the expectation that they will be processed to a finished and saleable state, and not at what they could be sold for at the reporting date in their raw or unfinished condition.

Even as regards current assets the validity of this assumption has been challenged, but its application to long period assets has aroused considerable controversy. [1] In effect, the continuity assumption leads to the valuation of assets such as buildings and machinery as unexpired costs, to be allocated against income to be earned in the future, and not at their present saleable price. The argument for adopting this approach is that, since there is no present intention to sell the plant, there is no reason to attach a saleable value to it, but it is recognised that the two recording assumptions conspire to allocate to assets of long life values which might be substantially different from "current" values, however defined.

The Construction of Financial Reports

Thirdly, there is a group of assumptions made in the construction mainly of published financial reports.

[1] A detailed consideration of the debate is to be found in Chapters 5–9 of this volume.

Most accounting reports are prepared for the guidance of managers and directors in controlling factors of production, or assessing past performance, or in decision formation. Internal management reports are as various in form and content as are the businesses and decisions to which they relate, and the only rules applicable to such reports are that they should, as accurately as possible, represent the underlying realities with which they are concerned, and that whatever assumptions are made in the construction of the figures should be clearly understood both by the accountant and the recipient of the report. There is no room in management accounting for inflexibility of approach, or for reliance on conventional modes of thought in financial reporting. Each report must be tailored to its specific purpose, and entirely pertinent to the objectives of management.

Freedom of design in accounting reports, whilst essential in internal reporting for management purposes, must be constricted in the preparation of annual or other periodic published accounting statements. Internal reports are prepared for executives familiar with the management problems of the firm, and are designed to assist in the resolution of those problems. Published financial reports, on the other hand, are used by a variety of people, investors, prospective investors, creditors, competitors and others, none of whom is concerned in the management of the firm, and each with a different focus of interest in the reports according to their existing or prospective financial relationship to it. In a sense, published financial reports must strive to be all things to all men, to depict the position and progress of the firm in such a way as to inform, and not to mislead, varied groups of readers whose information requirements are diverse. Furthermore, there are special problems attached to the preparation of published accounts. Unlike internal reports, which might be specific to particular problems, and cover whatever time periods are appropriate to those problems, published reports must refer generally to the entity as a whole, or to the collection of accounting entities which comprise a legal entity where there has been subdivision, and have reference to legally determined accounting periods, usually of one year's duration.

A part of the conceptual framework of accounting consists of a code of accounting behaviour in the construction of published financial reports, a series of rules which, if they have been conscientiously applied, and are known to readers of the accounts, limit the possibilities of misconstruction of the presented information.

Objectivity

Objectivity in accounting reporting connotes independence of judgement on the part of the accountant constructing the reports, and freedom from bias in representing the financial results and position of the enterprise reported on. Alternatively, it means that the published reports are capable of verification by a qualified person other than the accountant who prepared them.

It follows from the general concept of independent verification that as much of the content of financial reports as possible should be based on verifiable evidence, on values established by exchange transactions, and, wherever possible, such values are used. Thus long-term assets are shown in accounting statements at their cost to the entity, less aggregate depreciation to date, irrespective of the date at which the cost was established, and inventories of current assets are valued at ascertained cost, without regard to known present or likely future realisable values. [1] Objectivity, in this sense, means support by verifiable evidence, in contrast to subjectivity, which means dependence on the unverifiable opinion of the accountant constructing the reports.

It is seldom possible for all the figures in a set of published financial reports to be objectively evidenced. Some degree of estimation is almost always necessary, and in respect of estimated

[1] Where, due to external market conditions, the value of a current asset is *known to be less than its cost*, the implied "loss" is recognised in published financial statements. For a further discussion of the "lower of cost or market value" rule, see Chapter 6.

figures included in reports the concept of objectivity is satisfied if the estimates are based on all the available evidence, and constitute an unbiased view of the responsible accountant.

Consistency

A basic characteristic of the process of judgement is comparison, and the recipients of published financial reports, in making their several and diverse decisions, are entitled to an assurance that those reports are prepared on a consistent basis from year to year. Changes in accounting method, or in the assumptions underlying valuation procedures, could effect changes in reported incomes or financial positions without basis in fact, and the concept of consistency operates to limit distortions in reported figures by requiring that, in general, the same bases of reporting shall be used from year to year, but that if, in the interests of the introduction of better means of communication, changes are made, the fact that changes have been made and the effect of those changes on the reported figures should be disclosed.

Conservatism

There have been many instances in the past three centuries when the commercial community has been misled by over-optimistic accounting statements. Dividends in excess of those justified by earned profits have been paid. Valuations placed on such intangible assets as goodwill, royalties, patents and mineral rights have not uncommonly been too high. In a variety of accounting statements, but in particular in share prospectuses and published annual accounts, optimism rather than reality has sometimes been the basis.

Legal controls over published business data are now many and varied. Each new abuse has led to fresh legislation, but there seems to be no limit either to the optimism of businessmen or to the avenues for fraud which the growing complexity of the economy opens up. The first line of defence of investors and creditors is the vigilance of the practising accountant who, in most countries, is required to report on published accounting statements. Accountants, from long and sometimes bitter experience, are cautious men, and their caution is expressed in the concept of conservatism.

Conservatism as an accounting concept might perhaps best be described as an accountant's attitude of mind, but it can, in general, be stated that: if there is a range of values, each equally valid, which might be placed upon a profit or an asset, the accountant's tendency is to select one from the lower extreme. Conversely, if there is a range of values each equally valid which might be placed on a loss or a liability, the accountant's tendency is to select one from the upper extreme.

It is a usual accounting practice not to recognise profit until it has been realised. There are, however, instances when this practice cannot be followed. For instance, a major building might take several years to complete, and in each of these years shareholders in the building company will expect to be paid dividends. The concept of conservatism has a direct bearing on the accountant's attitude towards the valuation of work in progress, and consequently on the calculation of interim profits on uncompleted work.

It sometimes happens that, at the end of an accounting period, the extent of a firm's liability in respect of some matter cannot be calculated. For instance, a legal action which might result in the firm becoming liable to pay damages might be unresolved at the balancing date. Once again, in assessing liabilities, and consequently in determining profits, the accountant would tend to be conservative.

The overriding rule with regard to the presentation of accounting statements is that they should present true and fair views of profits and losses and of the financial positions of business enterprises. Conservatism in accounting practice means little more than that in assessing truth and fairness all due business prudence should be observed.

Disclosure

Modern company legislation prescribes in considerable detail the amount of information which must be disclosed in accounting statements. Although the rules vary somewhat from country to country, their general effect has been the development of the accounting concept that reports should present all the information which is material to an assessment of the business situation. Two points of interest arise here. In the first place, most countries prohibit secret reserves. Companies are not allowed to withhold from their shareholders information about the full extent of their assets. Propriety in accounting is very often a matter of opinion, and the accountant must tread warily along the narrow path between over-optimistic reporting in accounting statements, and unduly conservative valuations resulting in lack of disclosure of material information.

Accounts should not only present all the material information relative to a business situation; they should present it classified in a manner appropriate to the business. Totals and sub-totals of revenue and expenditure, and of assets and liabilities, focus attention on significant features of the firm's finances. Particular care must be taken to prevent misunderstanding through the aggregation of unlike items.

Not everything material to a business necessarily appears in the books of account. Accounting statements frequently need to be supplemented by reports by the directors on matters of concern within the context of which the accounts should be read. Failure to provide such information could result in the publication of misleading statements.

The Development of Accounting Theory

Accounting theory is not static; it is continually changing as economic conditions and legal rules alter. Nor do all accounting concepts enjoy unanimous support from members of the profession. Varying interpretations of many of the rules are possible.

The concepts which have been outlined are not more than a general framework within which the profession, in the exercise of its day-to-day duties, operates, but the search for better bases of accounting and for methods of financial reporting which will more adequately serve the needs of business and government is continuous. In professional society research departments and universities around the world the quest for a practical, and generally applicable, theory of accounting is relentless.

Discussion Topics

1. Accounting is a practical matter of recording and reporting on financial events. Why should a "conceptual framework" be needed, and what might be the utility of such a framework?

2. What are the practical reasons for putting physical and temporal boundaries on the accounting entity, and what are the major difficulties that arise in doing so?

3. "An account is only such if it expresses transactions in terms of money", but records are kept in other terms, and measurements in business are made in other units than money. However one defines *an account*, ought *accounting* to comprehend all records necessary to the information requirements of the entity?

4. "Subjective values . . . are undoubtedly useful in welfare economics; they have no place, however, in accounting" [Maurice Moonitz]. Why not?

5. What practical effects on financial reporting does the "continuity of activity" assumption have?

6. "Objectivity might be a desirable goal in financial reporting, but since accountants are human, it is impossible of achievement." Why?

7. Can a report be objective and conservative at the same time?

CHAPTER 4

Conventions, Doctrines and Common Sense*

IT HAS become almost habitual in expositions of accounting to offer some treatment of the so-called conventions and doctrines of accounting, and to regard these as the foundations or the theory on which accounting rests. The formal treatment and amplification of conventions and doctrines appears to have been introduced to the non-periodical literature in Goldberg's *Accounting Principles,* [1] published in 1946 as part of the post-war reconstruction training scheme. Subsequently they appeared in Fitzgerald's *Analysis and Interpretation of Financial and Operating Statements,* [2] in Yorston, Smyth and Brown's *Advanced Accounting,* [3] in Carter's *Advanced Accounts,* [4] in Mathews' *Accounting for Economists* [5] and in Carrington and Battersby's *Accounting.* [6]

In the first of these publications only four conventions (entity, continuity, accounting period and monetary conventions) and four doctrines (conservatism, consistency, disclosure and materiality) were presented. These were derived, as was the use of the terms "convention" and "doctrine" in respect of them, from Gilman's *Accounting Concepts of Profit.* [7] Fitzgerald did not

---

*An article by R. J. Chambers, first published in the *Accountants' Journal,* Wellington, February 1964, and reproduced by permission of the editor. R. J. Chambers is Professor of Accounting in the University of Sydney.

[1] Technical Publication No. 21, Department of Labour and National Service, Industrial Training Division, Melbourne.

[2] Butterworth & Co. (Australia) Ltd., 1947.

[3] Law Book Company of Australasia Pty. Ltd., 1947.

[4] Curtis A. Reid (Ed.), Pitman, London, 1956.

[5] F. W. Cheshire, Melbourne, 1962.

[6] Whitcombe & Tombs Ltd., 1963.

[7] The Ronald Press Co., New York, 1939.

produce the list completely, particularly in respect of doctrines. In his list of conventions he excluded the entity convention, substituted for the monetary convention as it was treated by Gilman and Goldberg a constant money value convention, added an historical record convention and retained the continuity (going concern) and period conventions. Yorston, Smyth and Brown (1947) retained the original list of conventions and doctrines, but in 1949 added to the list of conventions. The entity, continuity and period conventions were retained; the monetary convention was interpreted in much the same way as Gilman and Goldberg had interpreted it, though there were references to changes in the significance of the monetary unit; the historical record convention was retained following Fitzgerald. Two new items were added, the accounting equation convention and the recognition of law convention; but these were dropped in the 1963 edition. The new Carter presented the entity, continuity and period conventions following Gilman, the historical record and constant money value conventions following Fitzgerald, the equities or algebraic convention following the accounting equation convention of Yorston, Smyth and Brown, a new "arithmetic" convention, and omitted the recognition of law convention of the then current edition of Yorston, Smyth and Brown. The matching of costs with incomes was added to the list of doctrines.

Mathews noticed the entity, valuation, period, continuity and constant money value conventions, all of which he described as assumptions, and the doctrines of conservation, consistency and disclosure. Carrington and Battersby gave the largest list yet published: seven conventions—entity, valuation, period, continuity, constant money value, historical cost (following Fitzgerald of 1956), and recognition of law; and seven doctrines—conservatism, consistency, disclosure and materiality, all well established, and comparability, objectivity and economy, all introduced for the first time as doctrines. The 1963 edition of Fitzgerald appears to abandon the older structure altogether; it treats as assumptions the five imperatives of the "C" postulates of Moonitz[1] which, for the purpose of relating them to the established denotations, may be described as continuity, constant money value, consistency, disclosure and objectivity assumptions.

In all, the texts mentioned refer to ten named conventions and eight named doctrines, and in quite a few cases the connotations differ as between texts.

The Emphasis on Practices

In the light of these differences it seems timely to enquire what is meant by conventions and doctrines and what we have in their substance. It is instructive to go back to Gilman who, after a brief consideration of the meanings ascribed in several standard dictionaries, conveys the sense in which he understands these words and the ways in which he is prepared to use them. The characteristics of conventions are that they are propositions which are "based upon general agreement" and are "more or less arbitrarily established" (*op. cit.*, p.184). From the illustrations he gives, these propositions are descriptive of practices. Fitzgerald speaks of conventions as practices in a similar manner: "A convention of accounting is a practice generally followed . . . more often than not based on an implicit general understanding" (*op. cit.*, 1956 edition, p.8). As for doctrines, after considering these as propositions "taught by some persons" and as "a body or system of principles or tenets", Gilman concludes that a break with the implications of these dictionary phrases "would be a matter of considerable convenience"—a conclusion which is, to say the least, quite arbitrary. He chooses to use "doctrine" as "referring to a general statement of accounting or reporting policy" (*op. cit.*, pp.186–7). Fitzgerald does not find it necessary to break so obviously with the common usage of the language: "An accounting doctrine is a belief that a given practice should be followed . . . a dogma inculcated by teachers of accounting, textbook

[1] Maurice Moonitz, *The Basic Postulates of Accounting*, Accounting Research Study No. 1, American Institute of Certified Public Accountants, New York, 1961.

writers or authoritative association of accountants" (*loc. cit.*).

Now, it is a matter of fact that systematic studies of the ideas implicit in accounting practices have not a very long history. Paton's explicit statements [1] of forty years ago were not developed or even adopted by other writers, and it was not until the mid- and late thirties that interest reawakened. One would not wish, therefore, in any way to minimise the difficulties of any person wishing to give a systematic account of accounting, accounting ideas and accounting practices. Nevertheless, a few simple analogies will suggest that the form which has been taken by the texts cited, and in particular the emphasis on practices, is a form peculiar to accounting and should give rise to some doubts about its merits.

The practice of medicine involves such processes as diagnosis, prescriptions, surgery, and therapeutic care. But there are principles of medicine which are in no way dependent on practice; they are embodied in knowledge of the human organism and of the organisms and inorganic substances which affect it. The practice of law involves such processes as pleading and the assessment of evidence. But there are principles of law which are in no way dependent on practice; they are embodied in knowledge of the legally recognised relationships between persons. The practice of engineering involves such processes as designing and construction. But there are principles of engineering which are in no way dependent on practice; they are embodied in knowledge of the stresses which develop in and which may be sustained by structural materials and of the way in which materials may be combined. Examples can be multiplied. But in each case the principles are independent of practice. One may know the principles without ever having in mind the operations of diagnosis, pleading or building. One may expound the principles without reference of any kind to these operations. Truly there may be conventions in the practice of diagnosis, pleading or building;

---

[1] W. A. Paton, Assumptions of the accountant, *Administration,* June 1921, pp.1–17; and *Accounting Theory*, New York, The Ronald Press Company, 1922. In the former, eleven assumptions are given, only five of which appear among the conventions and doctrines of Australasian writers.

but these are peripheral and incidental, as the mere fact that they vary from place to place suggests. The heart of the matter is always something more substantial than the conventional forms with which practice is embellished or restrained; it subsists in the realities with which a particular kind of practice is concerned.

It seems to be quite otherwise in accounting. It appears to have become accepted that the ideas embodied in the conventions and doctrines of accounting constitute the fundamental or basic ideas for the field. The warrant for this inference is the fact that no other categories of ideas or of knowledge are put forward by the exponents of accounting as fundamental or basic to it. The conventions and doctrines are not peripheral or incidental elements of practice; they are all there is. All we have as fundamental or basic is thus a set of propositions which are more or less arbitrarily established or which are plain dogmas. There is no body of ideas or knowledge by reference to which we can judge whether or not these propositions are preferable to others; we must simply accept them.

This position is surely offensive to any inquisitive mind. And in any case it conflicts with common sense. For if there is a set of bodily conditions and disturbances which exercise the mind of a physician quite independently of the "conventional" bedside manners he adopts, surely there is an analogous set of conditions which exercise the mind of an accountant (as accountant and not as business adviser) independently of conventions. At this point the reader may interpose the suggestion that perhaps Gilman and his successors have simply made an unfortunate choice in the designations they have given to certain groups of ideas. But this choice was made quite deliberately, by Gilman at least. Nevertheless, we will examine the suggestion. Examination is not easy, however, for in many of the expositions there is no clearly identifiable proposition which unequivocally states what the author(s) mean. [1]

[1] T. K. Cowan's exposition, Notes of accounting theory, *Accountants' Journal*, Wellington, New Zealand, June 1957, is a refreshing exception. Each of his propositions is clearly identified by the introductory "that . . . etc.".

Some Conventions Examined

Consider first a convention which appears in all the quoted sources—the period convention. Yorston, Smyth and Brown assert that "necessity requires that in most cases [the] life [of the business enterprise] be divided into chapters known as accounting periods" (1963, p.12). Now, in the first place, the everyday and commonsense usage of the term "convention" implies some kind of agreement, and in an earlier paragraph it was noted that Gilman and Fitzgerald countenance the notion of agreement. One might expect, therefore, that the statement of a convention would begin in some such manner as "Accountants are agreed that . . . ". But the proposition quoted has not this form. It says "necessity requires that . . . ". If we are told simply that accountants agree to do a certain thing, and if we know that the accountants, in fact, agree, the proposition could not be further questioned. It would be a statement of fact and not a convention. When, however, the statement says "necessity requires that . . . ", we are bound to ask the nature of necessity, and what there is in the nature of necessity which requires that accounting periods be recognised. Necessity is said to be the mother of invention. May we then read: "The mother of invention requires that . . . "? The resulting proposition may seem ludicrous, but it tells us no less than the quoted proposition. If there is anything which requires periodical accounting, then periodical accounting is a consequence of that thing. And if there is such a thing, it is surely preferable to know it than simply to be assured that its consequence is a convention. The writer believes that the necessity of periodical accounting stems from a number of environmental factors, statements about which will lead to a conclusion of the form "If such and such ends are to be served, accounting statements will be prepared periodically". The necessity of periodical accounting becomes a reasoned conclusion, a status which is much superior to that of a mere convention. [1] Furthermore,

[1] For a demonstration of the argument, see R. J. Chambers, Detail for a blueprint, *Accounting Review*, April 1957, pp. 209–10.

most of the texts cited refer to periods of equal or fixed length. Good reasons may be offered for periods of variable length in some cases; and indeed some firms summarise results and plan operations for unequal periods. A convention which refers to periods of equal length states too much to be considered as a general rule without qualification.

Consider next the accounting equation convention. Carter does not state this convention in any clearly discernible propositional form. But the treatment given to it (*op. cit.,* pp. 4–5) has the form of an argument from certain premises and definitions. As we have just previously observed, the conclusion from a line of argument can in no sense be described as a convention. To do so simply results in the devaluation of it; for a conclusion based on argument from acceptable premises, that is from premises which conform with experience, is a far superior foundation of practice than something agreed upon more or less arbitrarily.

The recognition of law convention may be objected to, as a convention, on rather different grounds. We are told that "records and reports should give recognition to the legal position of the parties to whom the accounts refer" (Carrington and Battersby, p. 44). Are we to understand that accountants simply agree to abide by this proposition? And is it a more or less arbitrarily established proposition? Neither. Common sense suggests that the laws relating to the keeping of accounts are part of the environment of accounting. We do not consider all the elements of our environment to be simply conventions. We consider them as data, the facts of life. But, further, the authors go on to say that "it is frequently necessary to frame accounts in a manner that does not precisely display the legal position". And, indeed, every consolidated statement is a statement which does not display a legal position. Clearly, then, we are being told that accountants agree to give recognition to legal positions, and apparently they also agree not to recognise legal positions. What do they agree upon? If they agree upon both, then neither can be considered as a convention.

This leads us to another curiosity. Carter includes, as we have noted, the constant money value convention and the arithmetic convention. The former, we are told, "assumes that the purchasing power of money remains constant, which is not, of course, a fact" (p.4). In respect of the arithmetic convention we are told that "all the accountant's figure work is done by means of arithmetic; it is an obvious fact, and so is entitled to be known as a Convention" (p.5). Here we have two propositions designated conventions, one of which is a statement of fact and the other of which is contrary to a statement of fact. Quite apart from our objections to describing any statement of fact as a convention, what useful meaning can be ascribed to the term "convention" when it is used to describe such obviously different statements?

But consider more closely the constant money value convention. The sense of it may be conveyed in the form: accountants agree that, in the accounting process, changes in the purchasing power of money shall be ignored. Now if accounting were no more than a recreation, an end in itself as far as accountants are concerned, one could not perhaps cavil at anything they agree to do. But, if it were not obvious, there are countless statements in the literature to the effect that accounting is not a mere game for the delectation of accountants, that it and its products are "utilitarian in character" and "indispensable to modern business and finance".[1] As the usefulness of the information produced is a usefulness to other parties, it seems obvious that what accountants agree to do is not a matter of indifference—to themselves or to anyone else. Accountants are presumably no different from any other reasonable persons in attending to their own affairs. In budgeting their expenditures they do not think of the prices of bread, and cheese, and wine, in terms other than the prices they know to be relevant at the time. If they buy or sell a second-hand car they do not expect the sum initially paid for it to be relevant to themselves or to the seller or buyer. Yet, in respect

[1] Yorston, Smyth and Brown, 1957 edn., p.1; and Carter, p.1.

of the information they supply to other people they agree, in effect, that other people do not need, or shall not have, the up-to-date information which they themselves would require. They themselves need to adjust their affairs to the immediate facts of life, but apparently other people need only to adjust themselves to the facts as they existed weeks, months or years ago. Ethically and logically this is a most curious position to adopt. It requires more than mere convention to justify accounting on the basis of this notion. If there are reasons underlying the constant money value proposition we are entitled to be told of them in which case the proposition is a conclusion, not a convention. In fact, if usefulness is a criterion, common sense suggests that the reasons for accepting the proposition cannot be other than slight, if there are any reasons at all.

Sources of Confusion

It appears, then, that the term "convention" is applied to statements of fact, to statements contrary to fact, to conclusions from argument and to propositions of other kinds. Looseness of this kind can only mean that what is designated as a convention is itself quite arbitrarily determined. Without pure rote learning and indoctrination one cannot know what "accounting convention" means. For all its technical appearance, it apparently means nothing of a uniform kind which common sense would suggest we might expect of a term used in a technical context, even if it is also a term in everyday usage.

The doctrines are no less confusing and confused. Consistence in accounting is strictly a quality deducible from features of the world at large: its necessity stems from the fact that all judging and choosing, and therefore all action, involves comparisons, and the fact that valid comparisons can only be made of statements which are consistent or are derived by consistent principles. Disclosure means nothing more than informing, and that is the very essence of accounting. To give an account is to disclose. Accounting implies disclosure; nothing more need be said. And generally nothing more is said, except by way of giving illustrations. Materiality is nothing more than an informed sense of proportion. In everyday affairs we are quite accustomed to the kind of discrimination that is entailed. It therefore seems scarcely necessary to have an accounting doctrine to tell us to use our common sense. If the idea is extended to discrimination as between methods rather than as between results, it may acquire greater significance; Yorston, Smyth and Brown make brief allusion to such an extension (1963, p.17), but generally the illustrations given of its application relate to formal features of aggregative statements rather than to the quality of the information they convey.

All of this may be confusing enough. But the failure to state what authors mean by the conventions and doctrines they treat leads to greater confusion in the treatment. Only a few examples will be given. Yorston, Smyth and Brown, dealing with the continuity convention, state: "From the accountant's point of view, since the enterprise is to be kept continuously alive for the greatest length of time, financial and accounting policies automatically dictate that everything done is to be directed toward maintaining such continuity of activity; in other words, a policy will be undertaken conducive to nourishing the business for as long as possible" (p.12). It is difficult to see by what line of reasoning such a conclusion can be reached. Surely it is the concern of managers or owners to keep a business going, or to decide whether it shall be continued or abandoned. The only role accounting and accountants can play subsists in supplying managers or owners with information on which they can decide. Financial and accounting policies automatically dictate nothing; they themselves are dictated by or chosen because of circumstances and managerial preference. The only conceivable accounting "policy" is a policy of providing comprehensive and relevant information.

Again, we are told that the accounting period convention "necessitates accruing and deferring items of income and expense" (*idem*, p.13). There is no such implication. Entities which keep accounts on a cash basis also account periodically. It is true that if one does not account periodically the question of accruing and deferring items does not arise; but that is altogether different from the cited statement.

In a discussion of disclosure we are told: "If the basis of valuation of each asset is stated, persons reading the report are in a position to form their own opinions of the true meaning and significance of the report" (Carter, p. 7). But what sort of a position are they in? This statement implies that the report has not, in and of itself, a true meaning and significance; or it implies that "true meaning and significance" is only a matter of opinion. Disclosure surely means very little that is useful if the true meaning and significance of reports are not apparent and are only matters of opinion. In any case, how may the true meaning and significance be deduced from the stated figures and the stated valuation bases? Suppose that a company shows its commodity stocks at £10,000 and states that they are valued at "cost or lower", which is a very commonly stated basis. If the true meaning and significance of this valuation is not £10,000—and the quoted passage implies that this is so—how much better off is the reader for knowing that the valuation basis is "cost or lower"? No better off whatever. The value shown may be cost, £1 less than cost, or £1m less than cost: but the user has no means whatever of knowing. How, then, can he form any opinion about the true meaning and significance of the statement or the report in which it appears? No skilled accountant could do it; yet accountants are quite prepared to assert that persons generally can do it. If the quoted example is a fair illustration of what the doctrine of disclosure means, then it is an almost worthless doctrine.

Although no reference is made here to the periodical literature or to the English and American literature, it would be misleading not to point out that the kinds of confusion to which we refer occur also in that literature. Brief illustration may be given by reference to the continuity convention. Generally the meaning attributed to the idea is continuity of the accounting entity. But continuity is variously interpreted. Some speak of the enterprise remaining in operation indefinitely, [1] some of it having "a life expectancy greater than that of any asset which it now owns", [2] some simply of it having a continuous life. [3] Gilman refers to continuity of proprietorship, [4] and May refers to continuity of the accounting process. [5] Here is a series of quite diverse ideas masquerading as one; or at least having only one name. One wonders what respect would be accorded to physicians who had only one term for all diseases, or to lawyers who had only one term for crimes. To make one term serve for many concepts may be useful when all the separate concepts have been identified and labelled; but not when a general term is used sometimes to convey only one idea and sometimes to convey only one other idea. One other aspect of the matter is the explicit exclusion of the possibility that there may be any form of accounting for non-continuing entities. In many expositions the possibility is admitted, but it is brushed aside. Not even accountants treat continuing and non-continuing entities alike; so, if there is a convention to cover one type, in the interest of consistency and completeness there should also be a convention for the other type. [6] By implication a great deal of accounting is just ignored.

Oversights and Omissions

The conventions and doctrines, whatever they do assert, leave an enormous number of questions unanswered. They do not tell us why accounting exists at all. They do not say why it is necessary to conceive a business to be distinct from its owner(s). They do

[1] E.g. Carman G. Glough, Accounting principles and their application, *C.P.A. Handbook*, vol. 2; American Institute of Certified Public Accountants, New York, 1956, p.13.

[2] Smith and Ashburne, *Financial and Administrative Accounting*, McGraw-Hill Book Co. Inc., New York, 1960, p.50.

[3] E.g. Paton and Littleton, *An Introduction to Corporate Accounting Standards*, American Accounting Assoc., 1940, p.9.

[4] *Op. cit.,* p.81.

[5] G. O. May, *Financial Accounting*, The Macmillan Company, New York, 1943, p.49.

[6] M. Moonitz (*op. cit.*) is the only author known to the writer who specifically provides for both possibilities.

not give any rules or tests by which we may distinguish an accounting entity. They do not say why accounting is necessarily historic and not also anticipatory. They give no adequate reason for the preparation of two summaries, or for the form these take. They give no criteria by which the proper length of an accounting period may be determined in any particular circumstance. They do not tell us why some entities account on a cash basis and others account on an accrual basis. They do not tell us how to decide what is relevant information. They do not tell us how we may choose from among the multitude of valuation bases the basis which is appropriate in any particular·undertaking.

In the whole range of discussions of conventions and doctrines generally, there is no body of factual knowledge which is put forward as the foundations upon which practices are to be based. There is much talk, in accounting as in other areas, about knowing why as well as knowing how. But it is no advance in a man's knowledge if he asks why accounting summaries are prepared periodically, to say it is an accounting convention; nor, if he asks why follow the same methods from year to year, to say that is an accounting doctrine. If, on the other hand, one asks a surgeon why he makes an incision laterally or longitudinally he will explain his action in terms of the nature of the tissues, of the location of the blood vessels or the nerves, and of the nature and location of the organ he seeks. If one asks an engineer why he goes to the trouble to get structural steel in special shapes rather than flat or round sections, he will explain his action in terms of the improved resistance to stresses which special shapes possess. The actions of these people are made understandable by reference to the qualities of the things they work with. Knowing why in accounting can rest on no other basis than the qualities of the things accountants work with.

Necessary Fundamental Knowledge

What are these things? They are all observable and it is a relatively easy matter to make sensible and useful statements about them. It is not so easy to weave those statements together so that they provide a comprehensive foundation for accounting rules. [1] We are content here to list some of them briefly.

It is an observable fact that people seek to have accounting information so that their actions are the better informed. We should therefore understand the limitations of people which oblige them to seek such information. We should understand how people make choices and the part which habits, beliefs and verifiable knowledge play in the process. We should understand the part which valuation, estimation and measurement play, and the roles of experience and judgement in the selection of actions.

It is an observable fact that accounting is concerned with the economic aspects of actions. We should therefore understand something about the nature of the goods and services men seek to possess, of the processes by which they are transferred and of the media of exchange by which their transfer is facilitated. We should understand the different kinds of contexts in which actions are, or are to be, taken; and the different kinds of institutions for which accounting systems may be required.

It is an observable fact that accounting information bears on the actions of people in their relations with others. We should therefore understand the nature of co-operative systems, whether they are maintained voluntarily or contractually. We should understand something of the inducements and rewards of co-operation, of the nature and organisations and of the relationships between people in organisations, and between organisations themselves.

It is an observable fact that the processes of accounting involve the manipulation of numerical symbols. We should therefore know something of the nature of information processing methods and the problems of minimising losses of information in the translation of events to symbols and symbols to events.

It is an observable fact that accounting implies communicating. We should therefore know something of the nature of communi-

[1] An attempt is made in the author's *Towards a Theory of Business Accounting*. See Chapter 9.

cation processes, of the interferences which may arise when human interests are affected by what is communicated, and of the rectifiers which it may be necessary to build into a communication system to overcome these interferences.

Sufficient examples have been given to suggest strongly that there is an extensive range of knowledge, of facts, and principles, which underlies the practice of accounting. We can ignore them if we choose; we can be quite content with the vague notions which are described as conventions and doctrines. But to do so is to ignore the observable facts to which we have drawn attention, or to deny that they have anything to do with the case. In the name of common sense we can do neither. Intelligent persons in their relationships with the external world do not seek to resolve their problems by insisting that the world conform with their own image of it. When they find that the world cannot be made to conform, they are obliged to adapt themselves to a world of which they then have a better understanding. The brute facts of life cannot be met by conventionally accepted or arbitrarily adopted rules. If accountants are taught to think otherwise, so much the worse will it be for their future.

One cannot help believing that accounting must shake itself free of the very terms "convention" and "doctrine". They have hindered and obfuscated enquiry long enough, and as long as they survive they can do nothing but create the impression that accounting is a maverick among the professions and among the fields of knowledge. There can be no reason but self-destruction behind persistence in accepting arbitrary and dogmatic and authoritarian propositions which are formulated without regard for the realities of experience in the world at large.

In the place of the customary framework we must seek to establish a body of propositions which represent the context or the environment of accounting and to deduce from these in a rigorous, common-sense manner, even in a scientific manner, the principles and rules to which accounting should conform. In their personal behaviour accountants act in just such a way, as do all reasonable people: in their professional behaviour and in formulating their own principles, they cannot surely be satisfied to do less.

Discussion Topics

1. What do you understand by the terms "conventions", "doctrines", "postulates" and "assumptions"?

2. To what extent is "accounting theory" as expressed in the doctrines and conventions a mere expression in general terms of accounting practice?

3. "All we have as fundamental or basic is thus a set of propositions which are more or less arbitrarily established or which are plain dogmas." Does Professor Chambers overstate his argument?

4. "The conventions and doctrines, whatever they do assert . . . do not tell us why accounting exists at all." (Chambers.) Ought they to do so, and if so, how?

5. If accounting practice is a matter of knowing *how* to account, might accounting theory be said to be concerned with *why* we account?

6. " . . . the very terms 'convention' and 'doctrine' . . . have hindered and obfuscated enquiry long enough, and as long as they survive they can do nothing but create the impression that accounting is a maverick among the professions and among the fields of knowledge." (Chambers.) Discuss.

CHAPTER 5

Long-term Asset Valuation and Depreciation

THE Committee on Terminology of the American Institute of Accountants has defined the accounting concept of value: [1]

"*Value* as used in accounts signifies the amount at which an item is stated, in accordance with the accounting principles related to that item. Using the word *value* in this sense, it may be said that balance-sheet values represent cost to the accounting unit or some modification thereof; but sometimes they are determined in other ways, as for instance on the basis of market values or the cost of replacement, in which cases the basis should be indicated in financial statements. [2]

The word *value* should seldom if ever be used in accounting statements without a qualifying adjective."

In accounting valuations subjective considerations, such as the proprietor's opinion as to the value of an asset, are ignored. In general, *value* means historic cost to the accounting unit; assets and liabilities, income and expenditure are all accounted in money at prices ruling when transactions to buy or sell took place.

The cost concept of valuation causes some difficulty in the interpretation of accounting statements. A balance sheet, for instance, is not a statement of economic or realisable values, but of historic costs. The Cohen Committee outlined the conventional view. [3]

[1] *Accounting Research and Terminology Bulletins,* A.I.C.P.A., New York, 1961, Review and Résumé of Accounting Terminology Bulletins, p.17.

[2] The problems of revaluation accounting are dealt with in Chapter 8.

[3] *Report of the Committee on Company Law Amendment,* H.M.S.O., London, 1945. The opinion of the Cohen Committee on this point was confirmed by the Jenkins Committee in their report (H.M.S.O., London, 1962).

"A balance sheet is thus an historical document and does not as a general rule purport to show the net worth of an undertaking at any particular date or the present realisable value of such items as goodwill, land, buildings, plant and machinery; nor, except in cases where the realisable value is less than cost, does it normally show the realisable value of stock in trade. Moreover, if a balance sheet were to attempt to show the net worth of an undertaking, the fixed assets would require to be revalued at frequent intervals and the information thus given would be deceptive, since the value of such assets while the company is a going concern will in most cases have no relation to their value if the undertaking fails."

Balance sheet values ascribed to fixed assets are in no sense "economic" values or "realisable" values. They are the amount of the cost of assets which remains to be written off against revenue over the remainder of the expected life of those assets. Where an asset has suffered a loss of value, because of obsolescence for example, it is a matter both of accounting practice and business prudence to write down its value in accounting statements, charging the loss against current profits. On the other hand, appreciation in asset values (for example, because changes in the value of money have raised the saleable price of an asset above its depreciated cost) are generally ignored. This is an application of the concept of conservatism. Accountants usually provide for all losses, whether realised or not, but account for profits only when realised.

Fixed assets are thus usually shown in accounting statements at historic cost. The price paid for an asset is an accountable fact and, in this sense, balance sheets are objective: they are composed of "real" figures. Whether "real" figures are always also useful figures is, however, open to some doubt. Supposing a company shows in its balance sheet the following assets (ignoring, for the time being, the question of depreciation):

	£	
Land	20,000	(Bought 50 years ago)
Buildings	80,000	(£60,000 spent 50 years ago, the balance representing the cost of subsequent additions at various dates)
Equipment	40,000	(Various machines bought on average 5 years ago)
Stock	5000	(Many different items, bought on average 3 months ago)
Debtors	4000	(All expected to be good and to repay on average 3 months hence)
Cash	2000	
	£151,000	

Three significant points emerge:

1. *Each item in the list is a fact.* Every one represents actual money, or actual money paid or receivable. Except to the extent that there might be error or misrepresentation (for example, machinery might have been bought and charged against current revenue, thus reducing the equipment figure below total cost) the list is a factual statement of assets owned and prices paid.

2. *The total of* £151,000 *has no real meaning.* It is a summation of pounds of different values—pounds now, pounds 50 years ago, pounds 3 months hence and so on. It has about as much validity as saying that four apples and three pears equal seven fruit.

3. *The list of assets gives no indication of their present worth.* The land might be in a development area and saleable for £200,000. The cost of replacing the building and machinery in their present form might be £150,000. In fact, the assets might have a high present value or a low present value and, in consequence, the company might be rich or poor. But this is not revealed by the asset list.

The accounting profession has tended to take the view that statements of assets published in company balance sheets are records of the directors' stewardship over the resources entrusted to them by the shareholders. In a sense this objective is achieved. The balance sheet says "we obtained £X from the shareholders and others, and we have spent it on assets A, B, C and D having a total cost of £X". If the balance sheet had no utility other than as a proof of accurate accounting, and as a record of the disposition of funds, this would be satisfactory. In fact, however, shareholders, creditors, prospective shareholders, lenders and others are interested not in what assets *cost* but in what they are *worth*. The present stability of the company and its future prospects depend not so much on how it has disposed its resources in the past as on what are the present value and future potential of those assets.

On these matters accounting valuations in published balance sheets offer no guidance. Changes in price levels between the date of purchase of assets and the balance sheet date might completely invalidate the published figures except for the purpose of purely historic record. Facts are facts, but facts are only useful where they are relevant, and they can be positively misleading where they are irrelevant, and it is often the case that historic cost valuations in published financial statements are no longer relevant to the present business circumstances of the company.

Depreciation

The word "depreciation" has several meanings, among others being:

1. A decrease in value during some defined period:
   This meaning is the one most common in popular usage. It assumes the measurability of value either objectively as the "market value" of the asset, or subjectively as its "value to the owner", at two differing dates.

2. Allocation of cost:
   In this case the investment is regarded as a prepaid expense, to be allocated by some systematic method to the accounting periods encompassing the asset's useful life.

3. Shortfall from replacement cost:
   Depreciation is considered as the value difference between a new asset which might replace an old asset, and the saleable value of the old. It is the short-fall of the sale price of the old asset as compared with the purchase cost of the new one.

All the above concepts are useful, but each in different circumstances. The first expresses the general idea of depreciation as being a loss of value. The difficulty in accounting is to determine how much that loss is in monetary terms. The market value of the used asset might, or might not, be known, and even if it is known, might not coincide with the value of the asset to the owner, for instance, where the asset is an integral part of a complex production plant. Nor is it necessarily true that value to one owner must be the same as value to another. Imponderables of this kind render accounting measurement on the basis of this concept impractical.

The third concept suffers some of the disadvantages of the first: it assumes that it is possible to discover the saleable value of used assets, and furthermore infers that assets in current use will be replaced by similar ones when they wear out, which might or might not be the case. It is, however, useful when sale and replacement is in fact contemplated, when all the relevant factors can be quantified.

In accounting practice the second, or allocation of cost, concept is the most commonly used.

The American Institute of Accountants Committee on Terminology has defined depreciation accounting as follows: [1]

"*Depreciation accounting* is a system of accounting which aims to distribute the cost or other basic value of tangible capital assets less salvage (if any), over the estimated useful life of the unit (which may be a group of assets) in a systematic

[1] *loc. cit.*, p.25.

and rational manner. It is a process of allocation, not of valuation. *Depreciation for the year* is the portion of the total charge under such a system that is allocated to the year. Although the allocation may properly take into account occurrences during the year, it is not intended to be a measurement of the effect of all such occurrences".

The essential words are "It is a process of allocation (of historical cost) and not of valuation (of assets at current prices)".

Three factors determine the amount of depreciation to be charged. The first is the amount of the initial investment, and this can usually be determined with accuracy. The second is the circumstances which cause fixed assets to depreciate, and the third is the residual or saleable value of assets at the end of their useful working life.

Fixed assets depreciate in value for a variety of reasons. Most obviously, they are subject to "wear and tear" from actual operation. Even though repairs are made, especially to machinery, assets cannot be kept in perfect working order for an indefinite period. In addition, deterioration in physical condition might result from vibration, friction, strain, weathering or other things associated with the utilisation of assets. In some cases wear and tear are accelerated by careless use or inadequate maintenance.

Depreciation might be the result of mere lapse of time, where the period of ownership is limited, either by some rule of law or by contractual agreement, [but quite generally when an asset is no longer required by an enterprise for its original purpose, maybe due to the availability of equipment of an improved type, or because of a change in the productive objectives of the firm.

A special type of depreciation is depletion, which arises through the using up of such properties as mineral deposits, oil wells and forests. As a result of the extraction of resources the asset falls in value. Another is amortisation of the value of such assets as leases and patent rights, which depreciate solely as a result of the passage of time.

Expenditure on fixed assets is incurred for the purpose of obtaining benefits in future accounting periods. Depreciation accounting seeks to allocate that capital outlay to the accounting periods in which it is expected it will contribute towards the earning of revenue. Though each of the causative factors must be considered in determining provisions for depreciation, the resulting rates are not more than estimates made on the basis of the best evidence available at the time of investment. Neither the number of accounting periods in which an asset will be effective, nor its residual value are capable of more than estimation when depreciation rates are fixed on acquisition.

Suppose that a machine cost £20,000, and at the date of acquisition it was expected to have a useful working life of 5 years, and nil scrap value. If these estimates proved to be correct, £4000 would be charged to revenue in each of the years in which the machine was operative, and the objective of cost-allocation would have been achieved. It might be, however, that the estimates on which the depreciation rate was based are proved by experience to have been wrong. Thus, if at the end of the third year an improved machine became available, and it was decided to sell the original one for £500, £4000 would have been charged to revenue in each of years 1 and 2, but £11,500 would have to be written off in year 3. Alternatively, should the machine, at the end of year 3, be seen to have an expected further useful life of 5 years, the continuance of the £4000 per annum depreciation rate would leave 3 years "charge free". Even if the rate were adjusted, years 1 and 2 would have been charged £4000 each, whilst years 3 to 8 would be charged only £2000 each.

Depreciation is only as "objective" as the imponderables of future events permit it to be.

Depreciation and Income Measurement

Depreciation has been described (see p.67) as " . . . a process of allocation and not of valuation". As most accountants see it, it is purely a matter of apportioning the cost of long-term assets over the accounting periods which will benefit from their use.

A second, but by no means unimportant purpose of depreciation provisions, however, is to retain funds within the business to maintain the productive capacity of the concern. Continuing the illustration of the machine which cost £20,000 and had a life of 5 years, and assuming that the estimates at the base of the depreciation rate proved to be correct, the depreciation provision of £4000 per annum would:

1. Spread the cost of the machine over the 5 years to whose profits its employment had contributed, and
2. Retain from income £4000 per annum so that, at the end of the life of the machine, the original investment of £20,000 would have been recovered.

But suppose that, during the course of the 5 years, prices had so changed that to obtain new assets to replace the old one, so as to maintain the productive capacity of the business, would cost £30,000. Businesses are usually continuing entities and, when prices rise, depreciation provisions based on historic cost fail to retain in the business the funds needed to maintain productive equipment. In the case quoted, the £10,000 would have to be found from other reserves of the company or by raising fresh capital.

It is a rule in company law that dividends must be paid only out of profits earned, and never out of capital subscribed. [1] This is a sensible rule, having as its main objective the prevention of manipulation of share values by the declaration of dividends in excess of actual earnings. For example, in the absence of preventive rules, the directors of a company earning no profits might purchase blocks of the company's shares at a low price. A large dividend is then declared, the actual distribution being financed by returning to shareholders a part of their subscribed capital. As a result

[1] There are exceptions, but they are applicable only in special cases, and do not disturb the general validity of the proposition.

of the large dividend, confidence in the company rises, and share values go up. The directors thereupon sell their shareholdings and, besides realising a large personal profit, leave the company seriously deficient in assets.

Both legal rulings and accounting practice on this point have, however, concentrated on the preservation of the *money* investment of the shareholders. There is nothing either illegal or contrary to accounting practice in the failure of a company to maintain the *purchasing power* of the shareholders' investment. Suppose, for instance, that the opening balance sheet of a company were as follows:

Balance Sheet as at 1 *Jan.* 01

Capital (£20,000 shares of £1 each) £20,000 Machinery £20,000

The machinery has a life of 5 years, and depreciation is provided at the rate of £4000 each year. Profits earned, before providing for depreciation, are £8000 per year and a dividend of 20% is declared each year. At the end of the machine's life the position would be:

	£
Profits earned in 5 years	40,000
Less depreciation provisions	20,000
Dividends paid at 20% p.a.	20,000

Balance Sheet as at 31 *Dec.* 05

Capital (20,000 shares of £1 each) £20,000 Cash £20,000

Suppose it now transpires that the cost of new equipment adequate to maintain productivity capacity is £30,000, i.e. that money values have fallen by 50% over the 5 years. Clearly the depreciation policy of the company has preserved the money investment of the shareholders, but inflation has reduced the purchasing power of that investment. In effect, the dividends paid have been made up of:

	£
Surplus on trading	10,000
Payment to the shareholders of cash which should have been retained to maintain the purchasing power of their investment	10,000
	20,000

Where depreciation provisions are based on historic costs, accounting measurements of profit inevitably confuse trading profits and losses with the effects of changes in the purchasing power of money.

Accountants and businessmen are, of course, not unaware that normal depreciation provisions might prove inadequate to maintain the productive capacity of an undertaking, and it is common for special reserves to be set aside from profits to counter the effects of inflation. The amount of such reserves, however, is a matter for speculation about both the extent of likely future price changes and the possibility of technological developments which might alter either the productive process or the type of output of the firm. *If the proprietors had foreseen* the situation illustrated above, they might have met it by paying lower dividends, say 18% per year, when the £10,000 needed to maintain capacity would have been retained in the business.

Intangible Assets

Special problems arise in the valuation of intangible assets. Some, such as patent rights, can be treated in much the same way as tangible fixed assets, either the purchase or research cost of securing the patents being regarded as their accounting value, and charges to revenue being based on the allocation of that value over the legal or expected useful life of the patents. Others, however, defy objective assessment. Advertising and sales promotion costs are a case in point; they are incurred within specific accounting periods, but their effect on sales volume usually extends beyond the period of account. What proportion of advertising cost should be charged to revenue in the period in which it was incurred, and what proportion in subsequent periods must be based on a subjective assessment of the impact of the expenditure on the present and future revenue-earning capacity of the entity. Where a company engages in a continuous sales promotion effort, with the objective of establishing a more or less permanent product or company image in the public mind, some part of advertising expense might be regarded as capital expenditure, a contribution to goodwill, the intangible asset least susceptible to objective measurement.

Goodwill is the advantage and benefit of the reputation and good name of a business, the attractive force which brings in custom. Earning power is the dominant factor in determining the value of goodwill, and when goodwill is sold the price is a premium paid to secure an extra-profitable opening for the employment of capital.

The valuation of goodwill is one of the most controversial fields in accounting theory. There are conflicting opinions, and practice follows no generally accepted rules. When required to value the goodwill of an enterprise the accountant is working largely in the realm of conjecture, and is required to express an opinion on the future prospects of an enterprise, often with little factual evidence to guide him.

Apart from the capitalisation of advertising expense, goodwill is either ignored or shown at some historic cost calculated on earlier reorganisation or sale in the accounting statements of continuing businesses, but it is usually necessary to value goodwill when the financial interests in an entity change, for example, on the sale of a business, or its conversion to a limited company, or upon changes in a partnership due to death, retirement, etc., or when companies merge.

Methods used for valuing goodwill are:

1. *A number of years purchase of past annual profits*

This is a by no means uncommon, but decidedly arbitrary method. The choice of the number of years is a matter sometimes of convention in a particular trade or profession, and sometimes of agreement among the parties concerned. The basis of calculation is past results, and not future expectations, and the method does not automatically involve any consideration of the extent to which profits represent a reasonable return on capital.

2. *Capitalisation of estimated future profits*

This more scientific method places emphasis on the value of the business as a whole. It recognises that goodwill and tangible assets are linked together, and that the purchaser's primary consideration is the rate of return which the expected profits will earn on the price to be paid for the business. A person possessing a capital fund might obtain a minimum income without the possibility of loss by investing in a riskless investment, for example government stock. For the risk of committing his capital to a business venture, the purchaser expects to receive a higher return than he would obtain by safe investment. Goodwill might be said to be *the capitalised value of expected future profits less the normal profits which might be expected from that type of business having regard to the risk involved.*

The calculation of the value of goodwill on this basis begins with an estimate of the profits which the business is expected to earn in years to come. The estimate must be based on past profits, adjusted to reflect altered conditions which are expected to arise in the future. The second step is to ascertain the normal return which the purchaser would be entitled to expect from investment in this type of business, considering the risk involved. The greater the risk, the higher the return which will normally be required on capital invested.

Finally, the value of goodwill is calculated as that capital sum which, if invested at the appropriate business risk rate, would produce an annual income equal to the expected profits of the business, minus the normal profits of a business of that risk type.

The following example illustrates the methods of valuing goodwill which have been discussed.

BASIC DATA:

A.　Record of past profits:

	£
Year ended 31.3.00	2000
Year ended 31.3.01	1500
Year ended 31.3.02	4000
Year ended 31.3.03	5000
Year ended 31.3.04	7500
Average past profits—£4000	

B.　The rate of profit in the future is expected to be £5000 per annum.

C.　Net tangible assets are valued as at 1 April 04 at £20,000.

D.　Rate of interest considered necessary to attract and maintain capital in the industry—10%.

METHOD 1:

Goodwill = 5 (e.g.) × £4000 = £20,000.

METHOD 2:

Estimated future maintainable profit	£5000
$\dfrac{£5000 \times 100}{10}$ = Value of business	£50,000
Less value of tangible assets	20,000
Value of goodwill	£30,000

METHOD 2 (alternative calculation):

Expected future profits	£5000 per annum
Return which might be expected from net tangible assets of £20,000 at 10% per annum	2000 per annum
Expected return due to goodwill	£3000 per annum
The value of goodwill is the sum needed to ensure a return of £3000 per annum at an interest rate of 10%.	£30,000

It is not uncommon, where goodwill has been valued and entered in the books, for it to be written off out of subsequent profits. This is a somewhat illogical procedure, since, if profits are being made, the goodwill presumably still exists. If, on the other hand, no profits are being made, goodwill is valueless, but there is no source of income against which it can be written off!

Discussion Topics

1. "A balance sheet is thus an historical document and does not as a general rule purport to show the net worth of an undertaking at any particular date. . . . " (Report of the Cohne Committee.) What, then, *does* it purport to show?

2. To what extent is it true to say that published financial reports are records of the stewardship of directors, to whose management the shareholders' funds have been entrusted?

3. "The present stability of the company and its future prospects depend not so much on how it has disposed its resources in the past as on what are the present value and future potential of those assets." Discuss.

4. Why is the "allocation of cost" concept considered to be the most appropriate for use in depreciation accounting?

5. Depreciation can be charged on a variety of bases, per year, per hour, per mile run, per unit processed, etc. What factors might influence the selection of the most appropriate base?

6. Depreciation provisions based on historic cost preserve the money investment of the shareholders rather than the purchasing power of that investment. Is this justifiable in times of inflation or deflation of price levels?

7. "Goodwill is nothing more than the likelihood that the old customers will continue to purchase the old products." If this is true, can goodwill be said to have a "value"?

CHAPTER 6

Inventories

THE valuation of inventories of current assets raises a number of questions of accounting theory. The quantities and values of stocks of raw materials and finished goods, and the value of work-in-progress at the beginning and ending of accounting periods are relevant factors in the calculation of profits, and consistency in valuation procedure is clearly necessary if income calculations are not to be invalidated. The problem is to decide the bases on which the several kinds of inventory are to be valued.

The Institute of Chartered Accountants in England and Wales recommends that the following principles be applied: [1]

"The amount carried forward for stock and work in progress should be computed on a basis which, having regard to the nature and circumstances of the business, will enable the accounts to show a true and fair view of the trading results and the financial position. In most businesses the basis should be the cost of the stock held, less any part thereof which properly needs to be written off at the balance sheet date.

The circumstances of each business should determine the base which is appropriate and method of computation which should be adopted in determining cost and the part thereof, if any, which should be written off. In most businesses the choice lies between writing off any excess of cost over either:
(a) the net realisable value of stock, or
(b) the lower of net realisable value and replacement price; these terms have the meanings attributed to them below.

[1] *Recommendations on Accounting Principles*, no. 22, Nov. 1960.

76

In some businesses it may be appropriate to use special bases, including some which depart from the rule that profit should not be anticipated.

The basis adopted and the methods of computation should be used consistently from period to period. A change of basis or method should not normally be made unless the circumstances have changed in such a way that its continued use would prevent the accounts from showing a true and fair view of the position and results. When a change is made, the effect, if material, should be disclosed as an exceptional item in the profit and loss account or by way of note."

The following are the meanings attributed to "cost", "net realisable value" and "replacement price" in this recommendation:

(a) "Cost" means all expenditure incurred directly in the purchase or manufacture of the stock, and the bringing of it to its existing condition and location, together with such part, if any, of the overhead expenditure as is properly carried forward, in the circumstances of the business, instead of being charged against the revenue of the period in which it was incurred.

(b) "Net realisable value" means the amount which it is estimated as on the balance sheet date will be realised from the disposal of the stock in the ordinary course of the business, either in its existing condition or as incorporated in the product normally sold, after allowing for all expenditure to be incurred on or before disposal.

(c) "Replacement price" means an estimate of the amount for which, in the ordinary course of business, the stock could have been acquired or produced at either the balance sheet date or in the latest period up to and including the date. In a manufacturing business this estimate would be based on the replacement price of the raw material content, plus other costs of the undertaking which are relevant to the condition of the stock on the balance sheet date.

The comparison between cost and net realisable value or replacement price might be made by considering each article separately, or by grouping articles in categories having regard to their similarity or interchangeability, or by considering the aggregate cost of the total stock in relation to its aggregate realisable value or, as the case may be, aggregate replacement price.

Where the amount carried forward for stock is material in relation to the trading results or the financial position, the accounts should indicate concisely how the amount has been computed.

Opinion in the United States and Canada differs little from the recommendations of the English Institute. [1] The American Institute of Certified Public Accountants, in Accounting Research Bulletin No. 43, chap. 4 (1961), declared:

"The term *inventory* is used herein to designate the aggregate of those items of tangible personal property which (1) are held for sale in the ordinary course of business, (2) are in process of production for such sale, or (3) are to be currently consumed in the production of goods or services to be available for sale.

A major objective of accounting for inventories is the proper determination of income through the process of matching appropriate costs against revenues.

The primary basis of accounting for inventories is cost, which has been defined generally as the price paid or consideration given to acquire an asset. As applied to inventories, cost means in principle the sum of the applicable expenditures and charges directly or indirectly incurred in bringing an article to its existing condition and location.

Cost for inventory purposes may be determined under any one of several assumptions as to the flow of cost factors (such as first in, first out, average, and last in, first out); the major

[1] *Accounting and Auditing Approaches to Inventories in Three Nations,* Accountants International Study Group, 1968. Excerpts from paras. 1 and 2 read: "The first thing that strikes an observer comparing accounting and auditing practices in Canada, the United Kingdom and the United States is differences in terminology between the three countries. . . . On closer examination, however, the differences, at least so far as the subject of this paper is concerned, are seen to be largely superficial. Terminology may differ, but the underlying concepts are much the same. . . . "

objective in selecting a method should be to choose the one which' under the circumstances, most clearly reflects periodic income.

A departure from the cost basis of pricing the inventory is required when the utility of the goods is no longer as great as their cost. Where there is evidence that the utility of goods, in their disposal in the ordinary course of business, will be less than cost, whether due to physical deterioration, obsolescence, changes in price levels, or other causes, the difference should be recognised as a loss in the current period. This is generally accomplished by stating such goods at a lower level commonly designated as *market*.

As used in the phrase *lower of cost or market*, the term *market* means current replacement cost (by purchase or reproduction, as the case may be) except that:

(1) Market should not exceed the net realisable value (i.e. estimated selling price in the ordinary course of business less reasonably predictable costs of completion and disposal); and

(2) Market should not be less than net realisable value reduced by an allowance for an approximately normal profit margin.

Depending on the character and composition of the inventory the rule of *cost or market, whichever is lower* may properly be applied either directly to each item or to the total of the inventory (or, in some cases, to the total of the components of each major category). The method should be that which most clearly reflects periodic income.

The basis of stated inventories must be consistently applied and should be disclosed in the financial statements; whenever a significant change is made therein, there should be disclosure of the nature of the change and, if material, the effect on income." [1]

[1] Accounting Research Bulletin No. 43, chap. 4, is discussed in *Inventory of Generally Accepted Accounting Principles for Business Enterprises.* Paul Grady, A.I.C.P.A. Accounting Research Study no. 7, 1965, at p. 244 *et seq.* Grady adds (footnote 3, p. 251) "Standard costs are acceptable if adjusted at reasonable intervals to reflect current conditions so that at the balance-sheet date standard costs reasonably approximate costs computed under one of the recognised bases."

These are useful rules, but they leave substantial parts of the valuation process to the judgement of the accountant constructing the reports. It is the "circumstances of each business" which must determine the valuation base, and valuation might be in terms of unit, group or aggregate assessments. Furthermore, there are less obvious, but not less difficult valuation problems underlying the cautious advice of the professional societies.

The Cost of Raw Materials

The essence of the recommendations is that stock should be valued at the lower of cost or market price, whether market price is expressed in terms of realisable value or replacement price, but even in the simplest case, that of raw materials, it is by no means always easy to determine what might reasonably be called "cost".

It is usual for manufacturing, and some trading concerns to carry a large quantity of raw material stocks of varied types, and periodically to replenish these stocks to ensure that there is no break in production or trading due to shortage of materials. Since raw material prices fluctuate, there is no single unit price which can be allocated to holdings bought at different periods of time. This would cause no difficulty if raw material stocks remained unused in the warehouse, thus:

if 100 units of a commodity were bought in year 1 at £1 each, and

100 identical units were bought in year 2 at £2 each, and a further

100 units of the same commodity were bought in year 3 at £3 each,

the stock would have an aggregate cost of £600, and if neither disposal value nor replacement price were less than this, it would be shown in accounting reports at a "value" of £600. If, however, 100 units were used in production in year 3, or were sold, the accountant faces something of a dilemma. In that the units are identical, it is probably not possible, and in any case it is not necessary to distinguish physically those bought in year 1 from those bought in years 2 and 3. The problem is to decide what charge shall be made to the income account in year 3 for the stock used in that year, and correspondingly what is to be regarded as the value of the 200 units remaining in stock at the end of year 3. There are several alternatives, and reference is made to them by the American Institute, but it is seldom easy to decide which method will "most clearly reflect periodic income".

FIFO

FIFO (first in, first out) is a material costing system based on the assumption that the stock first bought is the stock first to be used. This assumption is seldom based on fact; if the units are physically identical and, as would most likely be the case, are stored together, the 100 units issued in year 3 in the illustration might be units bought in any year. Only where stocks are subject to deterioration over time is any effort made to marshal issues in purchase sequence. FIFO is, however, a reasonable assumption, and it can be argued in its favour that it keeps inventory values approximate to current prices. Thus the remaining stock at the end of year 3 should be shown in the published accounts at a "value" of £500. On the other hand, the FIFO base results in the issue of materials to production at historic, and usually lower than current, prices, with the result that if selling prices or tenders are cost-based, they will reflect past, and not present, material purchasing costs. If selling prices are independent of costs, reported profits become a compound of real trading gains and monetary gains resulting from the holding of stock over a period of rising prices. Thus, if the 100 units sold in year 3 realised £400, the profit computation on the FIFO base would be:

	£
Sales	400
Less cost of sales	100
Profit	300

but the £300 profit could be said to be:

A current trading gain of   £100
(The difference between the current buying and selling prices of £3 and £4 per unit respectively), and

A price-change affect of holding assets through an inflationary period of   £200
(The difference between year 1 and year 3 buying prices of £1 and £3 per unit respectively)

LIFO

LIFO (last in, first out) is a material pricing assumption precisely the converse of FIFO: it assumes that raw material stocks issued to production or sold are those most recently purchased. The effect of adopting the LIFO system is that inventories tend to appear in accounting statements at historic values, and, in periods of price increases, at values lower than present cost. Thus, at the end of year 3 in the illustration, the stock would be shown in the balance sheet as a "value" of £300 (the £100 spent in year 1 plus the £200 spent in year 2), though the current buying price of the stock would be £600 (200 units at a price of £3). On the other hand, LIFO incorporates current material costs in tendering and price fixing calculations, and tends to reduce profits shown in income statements to current trading gains. Thus, on a LIFO basis, the income statement for year 3 would read:

	£
Sales	400
Less cost of sales	300
Profit	100

During recent years the focus of attention among accountants has been on the income statement (or profit and loss account) rather than the position statement (or the balance sheet). The most accurate measure of profit has been considered of greater importance than the construction of balance sheets purporting to represent the present net worth of a business. It being that, in the matter of the valuation of raw material stocks, LIFO tends to support this approach, whilst FIFO tends to negate it, there has been a trend towards the adoption of the LIFO system.

Average Price

A third method of valuing stock is its average purchase price. Thus in the illustration the 300 units bought cost in total £600, and the average unit price is £2. Were the average price system to have been adopted, the 100 units issued to production or sold in year 3 would have been priced out at £200, and the profit calculation for year 3 would have been:

	£
Sales	400
Less cost of sales	200
Profit	200

There is little theoretical justification for the average price system. The value of stock shown in balance sheets is not usually an actual cost incurred at any point in time. (In the illustration, the balance sheet value would be £400, 200 units at £2 each, and £2 was the buying price in year 2. This is an accidental result of the simplicity of the illustration, but in any case only 100, and not 200 units were bought in year 2.) The system neither transfers price-change gains to revenue when stock is released, as does the FIFO system, nor does it withhold such gains from profit calculations as the LIFO system tends to do. It releases some part of price-change gains and retains the remainder in stock values, the amount released or retained depending on accidents of timing of purchases and sales of stock. The calculated profit of £200 is a compound of a current trading profit of £100 and an arbitrarily determined price-change gain of £100.

Despite its theoretical deficiencies, average price is frequently used in practice for reasons of accounting convenience. Both FIFO and LIFO result in sudden changes in stores issue prices; thus if 120 units of the commodity illustrated had been issued in year 3, 100 would have been priced at £1 and 20 at £2 under the FIFO system, and 100 at £3 and 20 at £2 under the LIFO system. Had average price been the valuation base, all the 120 units would have been issued at £2 each, and it is claimed in defence of average prices that they "smooth out" fluctuations in material buying prices, and avoid erratic changes in costs. Furthermore, it is usually the case that purchases of raw materials are rare, whilst issues are frequent, and whilst FIFO or LIFO charges require inspection of the inventory records whenever issues take place, average prices need adjustment only when purchases are made.

Standard Prices

A fourth alternative is to value raw material stock at its expected average purchase price over a fairly long period. Standard prices have no basis in transfer prices on exchange transactions, and require judgement on the part of the accountant and the purchasing staff, who must forecast the trend and timing of future price changes, and their use is, in consequence, not encouraged by the professional societies as a basis for inventory valuation in published financial reports. If standard prices are wrongly set, charges to revenue will under or over recover actual material costs, but if standards are reasonably frequently revised the amounts involved should be small, and there are substantial accounting advantages in the standard price system. If a standard price is the expected average material cost over a fairly long period, it provides a basis for both tendering and sales pricing which remains constant, and standard prices, since they change only when standards are revised, are as convenient in operation as average prices.

From the valuation point of view, standard prices tend to equate actual costs and charges to revenue over a series of accounting periods. In times of rising prices, standard prices will usually be higher than actual prices in the early years of the standard period, and lower in later years, both the raw material element in costs and the declared value of inventories varying around the mean in reports prepared for accounting periods shorter than, and within, the standard period.

A raw material cost in industry is composed of two elements; the price paid for the material, and the amount used in production, and standard prices effectively separate variations between actual and standard prices, which are the controllable responsibility of the purchasing staff, and actual and expected use of materials, the controllable responsibility of the production staff. Even when some other system of stores valuation is used for external financial reporting, [1] standard prices might be the basis of internal control over raw material costs and of production and cost reports prepared for the use of management.

Work-in-Progress and Finished Goods Stocks

The determination of what is the value of raw materials can, as has been observed, present difficulties, and there is almost always the need for the exercise of judgement in the valuation process. The value attached to work-in-progress and finished goods, however, is frequently of greater importance than that attached to raw materials, partly because these incorporate costs other than raw material, and thus have a greater cost-input per unit, and partly because in most cases the aggregate values of work in a partly completed state on the factory floor, or completed and awaiting sale, have a greater value than the aggregate of the values of raw material stocks awaiting entry into production. Both these factors depend largely on the length of the production cycle. If the period between the entry of raw material into production and its emergence as finished product is long, for example in heavy engineering, both the value added during production and

[1] Neither LIFO nor standard prices are acceptable bases for income tax computations in some countries.

the value of work-in-progress and finished product as compared with the value of raw material stocks will be greater than where the production cycle is short, for example in the fisheries industry. The valuation of work-in-progress and finished goods stocks introduces additional complexities, both practical and theoretical, into the process of constructing accounting reports.

The English Institute puts its finger neatly on the major point of difficulty in the words: "*Cost* means all expenditure incurred directly in the purchase or manufacture of the stock, and the bringing of it to its existing condition and location, together with such part, if any, of the overhead expenditure as is properly carried forward, in the circumstances of the business, instead of being charged against the revenue of the period in which it was incurred." "Expenditure incurred directly in the purchase or manufacture of the stock" is the sum of the raw material costs, however determined, and of wages and other outlays which are clearly identifiable with units of production. Some workers are engaged wholly on the manufacture of a particular product, some machinery is specific in purpose and there are other expenses which result in a measurable increase in the value of the raw material as it progresses to completion. It is not difficult to determine what part of these costs attaches to output which has been sold during the accounting period, and what part remains as an element of the value of finished goods stock and work-in-progress. Besides direct costs, however, and frequently a larger part than them of total costs, are indirect, or overhead costs; wages paid to supervisory staff or to ancilliary (e.g. maintenance) workers, the costs of machinery which makes a general, rather than a specific contribution to production (e.g. heating, lighting and ventilating equipment), and expenditure on administration, insurance, rates, social amenities, service departments and other such outlays, all necessary for the continuance of the productive process, but none of them capable of identification with specific items of production. How much of this expenditure should be incorporated in period-end valuations of stocks is a matter for the accountant's judgement, and whilst no one would quarrel with the

English Institute's advice that the amount should be " . . . such part, if any, of the overhead expenditure as is properly carried forward, in the circumstances of the business . . . ", the decision as to what is proper, and what are the circumstances of the business, depends on the assessment of the accountant in each individual case. Several alternative approaches are available to him.

Average Value

Suppose the output of a firm was 100 units, and the costs of production were:

	£
Direct costs:	
Raw materials (FIFO based value)	100
Other	200
	300
Indirect (overhead) costs	300
Total costs	600

Ninety units of the product were sold, at a price of £10 each.

One method of valuing the finished goods inventory is to prorate *all* costs[1] over *all* production (including work-in-progress, which, for simplicity of illustration, has been ignored in this example). If this were done, the profit calculation would take the following form:

	£	£
Sales		900
Cost of sales		
Output of 100 units	600	
Less value of closing stock	60	540
Profit		360

and the finished goods stock would appear in the balance sheet at a "value" of £60.

[1] Except selling expenses, which are normally written off in the year in which they were incurred.

Calculations on this basis are justified by the proposition that all costs are costs, each equally necessary for the continuance of production and that, in consequence, all costs contribute equally to output which is sold and output which is carried forward to a succeeding accounting period for subsequent sale. It is argued that it is immaterial whether costs are direct or indirect, in that the essence of a cost is not whether its impact on production is capable of identification with specific units, but whether the expenditure in question is essential for the continued operation of the firm. It being that, the rare instances of philanthropy apart, firms do not incur costs unless they need to do so, all costs incurred are necessary costs, distributable over sold and unsold output alike.

Direct Costing

An alternative argument is that direct costs represent expenditure on goods and services which have become incorporated in the product (product costs), and are therefore properly allocable as between sold and unsold output, but that overhead costs are period costs, incurred to maintain the productive capacity of the firm, and chargeable in whole against the profits of the period in respect of which they were incurred. Thus, it is argued, rents, rates, managerial salaries and the like have no utility beyond the accounting period during which the services in question were rendered, and no part of such costs should be carried forward as a part of the value of work-in-progress or finished goods stock. If this assumption were adopted, the calculation of profit illustrated above would be recast:

	£	£
Sales		900
Cost of sales		
Output of 100 units	600	
Less value of closing stock		
(10% of direct costs only)	30	570
Profit		330

The finished goods stock would appear in balance sheet at a "value" of £30, direct costs allocable to ten unsold units of output only.

Discretionary Allocation

The average value and direct cost systems are based on reasoning about the nature of costs incurred, but they result in the adoption of extreme positions in the valuation of work-in-progress and finished goods stocks. An intermediate approach is to consider each type of overhead expense, incorporating some in product costs and charging others against accounting periods as seems most appropriate in each case. This procedure introduces a further element of subjective judgement into accounting calculations, but it is not unreasonable to regard as "overhead expenditure properly carried forward in the circumstances of the business" such outlays as factory management salaries, the cost of ancilliary workshop machinery, lighting and heating charges, etc., which, though incurred in respect of periods of time, and not capable of association with specific units of output, nevertheless have a close relationship with the productive process. A common procedure is to value work-in-progress at direct cost only, but to attach to the value of finished goods stock an allocation of those overhead expenses associated with manufacturing operations, leaving administrative, selling and financial overheads to be charged in total to revenue as period costs. Though somewhat arbitrary in application, it can be claimed that this system, whilst attaching to work-in-progress no more than the value of its physical content, allocates to finished goods unsold their total *factory* cost, and that this is reasonable having regard to the probable low disposal cost of partly finished goods and the probable ex-factory price of finished product (less any profit element) if it could be purchased elsewhere. The use of this method would result in a profit figure somewhere between the £330 and £360 shown in the illustration of direct costing and average value, depending on the relative importance of factory and other overheads in total overhead costs.

Profit and Value

That accounting measurements of profit and value depend to a large extent on the discretion of the accountant charged with the duty of preparing financial reports is a constantly recurring theme of this volume. The extent of possible variation in reported figures can be illustrated from the examples used in this chapter. Either of the following calculations would fall within the generally recognised principles of accounting:

		Firm A			Firm B	
		£	£		£	£
Sales (90 units)			900			900
Less cost of production (100 units)						
Direct costs:						
Raw materials	(FIFO)	100		(LIFO)	300	
Other		200			200	
Total direct costs		300			500	
Indirect (overhead) costs		300			300	
		600			800	
Less value of unsold finished goods:						
(10 units)						
Direct costs		30			50	
Indirect costs		30			–	
		60	540		50	750
Profit			360			150

In the balance sheets the inventories would appear:

			£		£
Raw materials	(100 units at £2			(100 units at £2	
	100 units at £3)	500		100 units at £1)	300
Finished goods			60		50

The illustration magnifies the variability of profit measurements as a result of the adoption of different valuation bases, in that no opening inventories are assumed. In the case of a continuing business, and provided that there is consistency in the methods used, the opening and closing inventories would tend to cancel out in profit calculations if inventories held were reasonably constant in quantity and value over long time periods. Where there are substantial variations in the quantities of raw material

Year 2	Firm A £	£		Firm B £	£
Cost of production (100 units)			(100 units)		
Direct costs:					
Raw materials: (FIFO)			(LIFO)		
Opening stock					
100 units at £2	200		100 units at £2	200	
100 units at £3	300		100 units at £1	100	
	500			300	
Purchases					
200 units at £4	800		200 units at £4	800	
	1300			1100	
Closing stock					
100 units at £3	300		100 units at £4	400	
200 units at £4	800		100 units at £2	200	
			100 units at £1	100	
	1100			700	
	200			400	
Other direct costs	200			200	
Total direct cost	400			600	
Overheads	300			300	
	700			900	
Sales (at £10 per unit)		1000			1000
Less cost of production	700			900	
Add opening stock finished goods	60			50	
Deduct closing stock finished goods (10% of cost of production)	70	690	(10% of direct cost)	60	890
Profit		310			110

and finished goods stocks and work-in-progress held in a sequence of accounting periods, however, the choice of valuation bases can exert an important influence on calculations of profit, as is illustrated on page 91.

Year 3	Firm A £	£		Firm B £	£
Cost of production (300 units)			(300 units)		
Direct costs:					
Raw materials: (FIFO)			(LIFO)		
Opening stock					
100 units at £3	300		100 units at £4	400	
200 units at £4	800		100 units at £2	200	
			100 units at £1	100	
	1100			700	
Purchases					
300 units at £4	1200		300 units at £4	1200	
	2300			1900	
Closing stock			100 units at £4	400	
			100 units at £2	200	
			100 units at £1	100	
300 units at £4	1200			700	
	1100			1200	
Other direct costs	600			600	
	1700			1800	
Overheads	700			700	
	2400			2500	
Sales (at £10 per unit)		2100			2100
Less cost of production	2400			2500	
Add opening stock finished goods	70			60	
Deduct closing stock finished goods (⅓ of cost of production)	800	1670	(⅓ of direct cost)	600	1960
Profit		430			140

The difference in reported profit in year 2 (page 91) is entirely due to the different impacts of the LIFO and FIFO methods of valuing raw material stocks. The raw material cost of Firm A is £200, whilst that of Firm B is £400, and the inventory value of Firm A has risen by £600 (from £500 to £1100), compared with a rise in Firm B of £400 (from £300 to £700). The raw material costs of Firm B of £400 represent the raw material content of sales at current prices (100 units at £4). By using the FIFO method, Firm A has released £200 due to material price rises to revenue in the year of account.

In year 3 the price of the raw material is held constant at £4 per unit, but there is a substantial difference between sales and output. The effect is as on page 92.

The difference of £290 between the two profit figures consists of £100 in different raw material charges (£1100 in Firm A and £1200 in Firm B) and £200 in the different amounts of overhead cost retained in closing stock inventories in the two firms. Thus Firm A has valued its closing stock of finished goods at £800, one-third of total costs of £2400, whilst Firm B has taken £600, one-third of direct costs only. (The remaining £10 of the difference lies on the values attributed to opening stocks of finished goods.)

Neither Firm A nor Firm B could be accused of violating recognised accounting principles in computing their profits, and arguments can be adduced in support of both procedures, yet their results are very different. Deciding what is appropriate to the "circumstances of each business" is not a problem which lends itself to easy solution.

Discussion Topics

1. The valuation of inventories on the basis of lower of cost or market value is justified on the grounds that losses should be recognised in the accounts as soon as they are evidenced, but that profits should not be accounted until they are realised by a sales transaction. Is this a sensible rule of business prudence or a case of undue conservatism in the measurement of income?

2. Because the last in, first out system of inventory pricing tends to match current costs against current revenues in the measurement of income it is favoured by many accountants. Its use is, however, not permitted in income tax computations in many countries. Why might this be so?

3. "There is little theoretical justification for the average price system." Then why should anyone use it?

4. What are the advantages and disadvantages of standard prices for inventory valuation?

5. "'Cost' means all expenditure incurred directly in the purchase or manufacture of the stock" (Recommendation 22 of the English Institute), but what does "directly" mean?

6. " . . . the choice of valuation bases can exert an important influence on calculations of profit. . . . " Discuss, with reference to both long-term assets and inventories.

CHAPTER 7

The Measurement of Income

As was explained in Chapter 3, there are legal and economic reasons why the income [1] of entities must be measured annually for the information of shareholders, creditors, tax gatherers and others, irrespective of whether the calendar year is a time division appropriate to the production and exchange circumstances of the entity, but the periodic measurement of income for the purposes of public reporting presents accountants with some of their most difficult problems.

An obvious approach would be by way of the comparison of the net worth of an entity at the beginning and ending of the accounting period. Thus, if the assets less non-proprietary interests in an entity on 1 January had a value of £10,000, and one year later a value of £15,000, the income of the entity, assuming that there had been no infusions or withdrawals of capital by entity owners, would be £5000. Alternatively, it might be said that the interest of the proprietors in the entity had risen by £5000. Accountants often use this method when seeking to measure the income of small traders or unincorporated social organisations when adequate accounting records have not been kept, but even in small businesses difficulties of calculation arise, and in the case of a large concern comparison of net worth as a means of income measurement would not be practical, despite theoretical attractions.

Comparisons of net worth necessarily require that net worth be measured, and herein lies the difficulty. In one sense, an entity has value because of its ability to provide a future flow of income; thus if the net assets of a business at a point in time were deemed

[1] Or net profit.

capable of producing an income of £5000 per year for 10 years, after which they would be valueless, it could be said that their present value is £50,000. This is, however, an unrealistic simplification of actual business circumstances. Entities do not usually contain a homogeneous collection of assets with equal life spans, they consist of a variety of assets with different life spans, and the quality and quantity of assets within an entity is subject to continuous change. The heterogeneous nature of business assets alone would make the calculation of future income difficult, but there are other factors to be considered. Entities seldom have a known date of termination when accounting reports are constructed, hence the estimation of future income ought to extend into a seemingly limitless future. Future income, moreover, is not solely a function of the net assets of the business; it depends on future market conditions for both inputs and outputs, and these can rarely be predicted with any certainty, even for short future periods. It is not, in consequence, except in quite special conditions, possible to establish what the future earnings of an entity might be without engaging in hazardous speculation about the direction of future events, but even if it were possible, there remains another problem. Income receivable in the future is not as desirable as income receivable today: if £1000 held now were invested at 5% it would accumulate to £1050 in one year's time—£1000 now would be worth £50 more a year hence than £1000 receivable then, and future income, if it could be calculated, would need to be discounted if its present value were to be included in a computation of net worth. What rate of discount to use, however, is not obvious—it might be the present risk-free lending rate, or the risk-free lending rate expected to be effective when the income is earned, or a present or future risk-loaded rate, or . . . . Nor is this all. Money has a tendency to depreciate in value, but what assumptions one ought to make about the purchasing power of future money as compared with the purchasing power of present money is a matter of pure conjecture.

Since the calculation of net worth on the basis of future income-potential raises so many problems capable of resolution only by subjective judgement, a profit measurement based on net worth at period ends could hardly be claimed to be more than an unverifiable opinion resting on assumptions about quite unpredictable future events.

An alternative way of seeking to approximate asset values shown in published financial statements to present net worth is by periodic revaluation of assets to realisable or replacement cost. Procedures of this kind are, in fact, used by some organisations, but they, too, involve a considerable amount of subjective judgement on the part of the accountant, [1] and usual practice is to base accounting measurements of income on a comparison of the revenue arising in an accounting period with the costs incurred in that, or previous periods, associated with the earning of that revenue. Though by no means wholly objective, income measurement through the matching of costs and revenues avoids the more difficult problems of estimation inherent in other methods.

Matching Costs with Revenues

Accounting measurements of income focus attention not on the difference between net worth at two points in time, but on the reasons why changes in net worth take place. It is argued that the net worth of an entity increases or reduces over a period of account because revenue is greater or less than cost during that period, and the basic reason for the accountants' choice of method is that revenue and costs are more susceptible to objective measurement than is net worth. Since net income is normally calculated at the end of an accounting period, the revenues and costs to be matched are *past* revenues and costs, all evidenced by exchange transactions which took place either during the period or earlier. This is not to say that accounting measurements of income are "true", but only that they are verifiable, nor is it to say that there is a unique accounting measurement of income for each entity in each accounting period. Even though dealing with historic and evidenced data, the accountant cannot escape the exercise of

[1] Revaluation accounting is discussed in Chapter 8.

discretion in a number of significant areas of the income measurement process. Income is calculated by deducting from revenue all costs incurred in earning that revenue, and the calculation depends on assumptions concerning the recognition of costs and revenues —the points in time when costs are accounted as having been incurred and revenues are accounted as having been earned, and the methods by which costs are identified with the revenues to which they are relevant.

The Recognition of Revenues and Costs

It would be possible to recognise revenue by bringing it, as such, within the compass of a periodic income statement[1] at a variety of points in the typical transaction history. Thus the point of sale might be regarded as the occasion when the order for goods or services was received, or when the goods were delivered or the services rendered, or when the transaction was completed by the receipt of cash. To recognise revenue on receipt of an order is to adopt the most optimistic attitude, to assume that the whole transaction will proceed as planned to its termination in the receipt of cash, and this basis is seldom used. Sales transactions do not always run their expected course—goods despatched might be returned as unsuitable, the terms and conditions might be altered, and the debtor might fail to meet his obligation to pay. In general, the receipt of an order is regarded as being too early in the history of a transaction for there to be enough evidence of its successful completion to warrant that point in time being selected for the accounting recognition of revenue.

Recognition of revenue when cash is received is the least optimistic assumption to adopt. It has the merit of being the most objective (transactions are not recognised until all the facts are known) and is appropriate in use where the great majority of sales is on a cash basis, in a cash-only retail business or a public transport utility, for example. In general, however, to defer the recognition of revenue until the receipt of cash would distort

[1] Or revenue account, or profit and loss account.

periodic income measurements because it is normal trade practice for cash settlement to be effected some time after goods have been delivered or services rendered; the productive effort is not coincident in time with the receipt of cash where sales, as is usual, are on a credit basis. Governments usually prepare their accounts on a cash basis, but their objectives are the management of national economies rather than the production of goods and services, and for this purpose cash-flow accounting is believed preferable, and small social clubs frequently keep cash accounts only because the volume of transactions does not justify the use of some more elaborate system, but these exceptions apart, the receipt of cash is regarded as too late a point in the process of a sales transaction for the recognition of revenue.

Usual practice is to recognise revenue when goods are delivered or services are rendered. This is the point in time when the productive process has ended by the delivery of goods or the provision of a service, when the goal of an entity, to sell its output, has been achieved. It is also the point in time when the association between the supplier and the customer crystallises into a creditor–debtor relationship, when there is a change in the physical possession of goods and in the legal rights of the parties to the transaction. Recognition of revenue when goods are delivered or services rendered leaves only one element of the transaction process unverified, the ultimate cash settlement of the debt, and it is usual to deal with this matter by the inclusion in income calculations of an overall provision for uncollectable accounts.

All the arguments relevant to the recognition of revenue apply with equal force to the recognition of costs. Thus a cost could be recognised when goods or services were ordered, or when they were received or performed, or when cash was paid out in settlement. Quite apart from the desirability of consistency of treatment of both costs and revenues, the weight of evidence favours the recognition of costs, as of revenues, at the point of delivery of goods or the rendering of services.

The Matching Process

The matching process begins with the determination of the revenue for the accounting period, the revenue against which costs are to be matched. In most cases this occasions little difficulty: revenue is the total of the sales prices of all goods delivered or services rendered in the period. Most of the difficulties encountered in the matching process arise in deciding which costs, or how much of some costs, are to be regarded as applicable to the determined revenue of the period. The basic principle is that there should be matched with revenue all those costs incurred in acquiring goods or services whose utility has expired in the earning of that revenue. Where the utility of a good or service has only partially expired, that part of its cost which is relevant to the operation of the entity in the accounting period should be included in the income computation for the period, the remainder being carried forward as an unexpired cost for matching against the revenues of subsequent periods.

Consideration of what is, and what is not an expired cost was, indirectly, the subject matter of most of Chapters 5 and 6. Long-term assets might be defined as assets having an expectation of useful service in an entity longer than a single accounting period and, from the viewpoint of matching costs with revenues, the whole process of depreciation accounting can be regarded as one of deciding which parts of the cost of long-term assets expire in which periods of account. Similarly, the "value" at which long-term assets are shown in accounting statements represents unexpired cost, that part of the original cost of the assets representing services as yet unused at the balance sheet date. Thus the American Institute of Accountants Committee on Terminology declared (see p.66):

> "*Depreciation accounting* is a system of accounting which aims to distribute the cost or other basic value of tangible capital assets . . . over the estimated useful life . . . in a systematic and rational manner. *Depreciation for the year* is the portion

of the total charge under such a system that is allocated to the year."

As was pointed out in Chapter 5, there are many imponderables in depreciation accounting, and there is no single method which is "systematic and rational" in the circumstances of all businesses, or even in the circumstances of one business. The cost of long-term assets matched against the income of a period of account depends on calculations involving subjective judgements about the future service lives of assets and their terminal realisable values.

Also discussed in Chapter 5 was the question of advertising expense, and the extent to which such outlays have effect only on the revenue of the accounting period in which they were incurred, or also on the revenues of subsequent periods, or even on the permanent selling potential of the firm through their impact on goodwill. Once again, this is a question of expired or unexpired costs. Some advertising expense is readily amenable to classification, thus the cost of short-period advertisement of a "special offer" clearly expires when the "special offer" ceases to be available, and cumulative expenditure designed to build up a permanent brand name for a product might have such a long-term effect on the entity's market position as to merit its capitalisation as goodwill. Between these extremes, however, lies an area where accounting policy must depend on judgement, and the not uncommon practice of treating all except long-term brand image advertising costs as period costs, expiring at the point of expenditure, though convenient and prudent, is a distortion of the fundamental concept of matching costs against revenues.

Chapter 6 dealt in detail with the question of what is the "cost" of raw materials, and it was demonstrated that the adoption of different valuation assumptions might result in different material costs being matched against revenues in the determination of periodic income. Furthermore, there are alternative approaches to the question of how much overhead cost shall be incorporated in period-end inventories of work-in-progress and finished goods (and therefore regarded as unexpired costs), and how much shall be charged to revenue as expired costs in the period in which they were incurred. Once again, there is scope for judgement, and for difference of opinion among accountants.

The discretionary elements in the process of matching costs against revenues, as they have been discussed in the preceding chapters, are summarized in the following example.

Income Statement for year ended 31 *March*

	£	£	£
Sales			100,000
Cost of production			
Raw materials			
Opening stock (Note 1)	3000		
Purchases	40,000		
	43,000		
Less closing stock (Note 1)	5000		
	38,000		
Other direct costs (Notes 2 and 3)	32,000		
Total direct cost	70,000		
Add opening work-in-progress (Note 4)	10,000		
	80,000		
Less closing work-in-progress (Note 4)	8000		
	72,000		
Factory overheads (Note 3)	8000		
		80,000	
Add opening finished goods stock (Note 4)		8000	
		88,000	
Less closing finished goods stock (Note 4)		6000	
Cost of sales			82,000
Gross income			18,000
Administrative, financial and other overheads (Note 3)			8000
Net income			10,000

Note 1. The value attributed to stocks of raw materials depends on the meaning attributed to the words *lower of cost or*

market and in particular on the choice of the pricing system, whether last in, first out, first in, last out, average, or some other.

Note 2. The decision as to what is a direct cost and what is a part of factory overhead is not always clear, and often depends on the extent to which it is deemed necessary to maintain special records. Thus meters might be installed to trace the consumption of electricity to each productive part of the factory, when electricity charges could be included in direct costs as being directly associated with the production of specific output, or a single meter might record overall factory consumption, when electricity charges would be included in factory overhead.

Note 3. Long-term assets are diverse in nature, and they might make a direct contribution to output (e.g. where a machine is specific in purpose, and wholly employed on the production of a single type of output), or a general contribution to production (e.g. factory buildings), or a contribution to the administration of the firm (e.g. office buildings and machinery). It is sometimes the practice to include all factory long-term asset costs in factory overhead, retaining only short-period costs in direct costs, but whether this is done or not, the cost of long-term assets matched against revenue in the income statement depends on the assumptions adopted concerning asset valuation and depreciation method.

Note 4. The values attributed to stocks of work-in-progress and finished goods depend on the meaning attributed to the words *lower of cost or market value*, and in particular on the extent to which overhead costs are regarded as unexpired, and are included in those values.

An income measurement derived from a comparison of costs and revenues is essentially historic, a comparison of past revenues with past costs; the objective of accounting measurements of income is evaluation of the past performance of the entity, on the basis of which dividends or other payments to owners might be made. Some consideration of future events is inescapable even in the measurement of past income, thus depreciation rates depend on unknown future asset lives and disposable values, but as few predictions, and as many facts as possible is the guiding rule. No doubt many of those who read accounting reports are more interested in the future than in the history of an entity— their conduct depends on what they believe the future course of events is likely to be, and it is sometimes suggested that accounting measurements of income would have greater utility if they had regard to the continuing progress rather than the past achievement of the entity. On the other hand, it can be argued that speculation is the business of the speculator, and that his predictions are better founded on factual records of the past than on unverifiable opinions about future events in accounting reports.

The Income Statement and the Balance Sheet

An income statement and a balance sheet are not independent documents. It was suggested early in this chapter that one measurement of income might be derived from a comparison of the net worth of an entity at two points in time or, in balance sheet terms:

$$(A1 - L1) - (A0 - L0) = I(0 \text{ to } 1) \ or$$
$$NW(1) - NW(0) = I(0 \text{ to } 1),$$

where A means gross assets, L means liabilities other than owners' equity, I means net income, NW means net worth (or owners' equity) and 0 to 1 are two points in time. The matching process is based on the proposition that:

$$I(0 \text{ to } 1) = R(0 \text{ to } 1) - C(0 \text{ to } 1),$$

where R means revenue and C means costs. The relationship between the two statements can be demonstrated as:

$$NW(1) - NW(0) = I(0 \text{ to } 1),$$
$$or \ NW(1) - NW(0) = R(0 \text{ to } 1) - C(0 \text{ to } 1),$$
$$or \qquad NW(1) = NW(0) + [R(0 \text{ to } 1) - C(0 \text{ to } 1)].$$

Net worth at point 1 consists of net worth at point 0 plus revenues earned less costs incurred during the period 0 to 1.

The objective of the balance sheet is to display the financial position of an entity at balance date, whilst the revenue account is concerned with the revenues received and the costs incurred between balance dates, but neither net worth nor net income are capable of precise determination. Because balance sheets and net worth are directly related to income statements and net income, assumptions made in the construction of either document must be reflected in the other. Two approaches are possible. The first is to emphasise the balance sheet as a statement of net worth, to seek to place values on assets and liabilities which will make the document a valid record of the financial position and potential of the entity at balance date. If this were done, the income statement would be required to do more than account for historic cost transactions in explaining how changes in net worth between balance dates had come about. The difficulties inherent in this approach were discussed at the beginning of this chapter; in summary there are so many imponderables involved in the computation of net worth that it is doubtful if a balance sheet of economic utility could be constructed, or if income could be computed on the basis of a comparison of period-end position statements.

Because of the problems associated with balance sheet construction, there has been a tendency to place emphasis on the income statement in accounting reporting. The process of matching costs against revenues, despite the difficulties involved, is an acceptable means of measuring income for dividend and taxation purposes, but the assumptions necessarily adopted in the construction of the income statement have had the effect of reducing the balance sheet to little more than a schedule of unexpired costs, set against a statement of external debt, with owners' equity as the residual figure. Thus depreciation accounting has as its object the matching of the costs of long-term assets against the revenues earned through the employment of those assets, a procedure entirely appropriate to the objectives of the income statement, but the "values" attached to long-term assets in balance sheets, as a result, are no more than unexpired costs awaiting allocation to the income accounts of subsequent periods.

It is not possible, because of our inability to predict the pattern of future events, for an acceptable measure of past income and a statement of present worth of economic utility to be presented in a single series of articulated accounting statements, and as a matter of priority, the income statement usually has precedence over the balance sheet.

Special Cases in Matching Costs and Revenues

In most entities, the determination of cost is the area in which the majority of matching problems arise. Sometimes, however, there are difficulties in the allocation of revenue to accounting periods. This is so where the productive process is longer than the period of account, for example in building and other construction work, heavy engineering and shipyards, where purchasers usually undertake by contract to make progress payments to the productive entity as work proceeds. This is a special case of an accounting period inappropriate to the productive circumstances of a business, but, since such businesses are usually engaged in a number of projects, with different time spans, the likelihood is that *no* accounting period would be appropriate. The usual procedure is to treat progress payments as revenue, calculating income by matching against the payments such costs as are relative thereto, and reserving an appropriate sum for contingencies.

Contract price £50,000
Payable £20,000 on completion of Stage 1
£20,000 on completion of Stage 2
£10,000 on completion of the project

At the end of the first accounting period Stage 1 had been completed, and Stage 2 was partly completed.

	£	£
Revenue (progress payment for Stage 1)		20,000
Costs incurred to date	18,000	
Less costs applicable to Stage 2, carried forward to be matched against the Stage 2 progress payment	1000	17,000
Gross income from contract to date		3000
Less provision for contingencies (claims for faulty work, unforeseen structural difficulties, etc.)		2000
Net income from contract to date		1000

The £1000 expended on work applicable to Stage 2 is carried forward in the balance sheet as an unexpired cost, no income being accounted in respect of the outlay, and this together with the provision for contingencies, results in a somewhat conservative measurement of income. An alternative approach is to compute revenue on the basis of incurred costs to date. If this method were used, the income for the first accounting period would be calculated:

	£
Costs incurred to date	18,000
(Expected total costs on the contract are £40,000)	
Revenue: $\dfrac{£18,000}{£40,000} \times £50,000$	22,500
Gross income from contract to date	4500
Less provision for contingencies	2000
Net income from contract to date	2500

In this calculation, revenue of £2250 which has not become due for payment under the contract is included in income, and all costs incurred to date are regarded as expired. While neither method is theoretically objectionable, the second would clearly be appropriate only where the total costs to be incurred on the project are capable of ascertainment with some exactitude, and where there is no doubt about the ability of the contractee to meet his progress payment liabilities as they fall due.

A further special case of income measurement arises where sales are made on the basis of instalment payments, whether by hire-purchase agreement or through arrangements for deferred credit. Two approaches are possible. The whole of the income from the sale might be accounted in the period in which the transaction took place, adequate reserves for possible bad debts being made, or the costs and revenues associated with the transaction might be prorated over the payment period.

Goods costing £10,000 were sold for £15,000, £3000 to be paid in each of 5 years. The purchaser paid the first four instalments, but defaulted on the last. The goods were recovered in year 5, and were found to have a scrap value of £1000.

METHOD 1

		£
Year 1	Revenue	15,000
	Costs	10,000
	Gross income	5000
	Less provision for doubtful debts	2000
	Net income	3000
Year 5	Revenue (scrap value of goods)	1000
	Costs (bad debt acknowledged)	3000
	Gross loss	2000
	Transfer from provision for doubtful debts	2000
	Net income	—

METHOD 2

	Revenue	Costs	Net income	Costs carried forward for matching with subsequent income
	£	£	£	£
Year 1	3000	2000	1000	8000
2	3000	2000	1000	6000
3	3000	2000	1000	4000
4	3000	2000	1000	2000
5	1000	2000	−1000	—

The first method follows the basic matching procedure of accounting costs and revenues in the period in which physical possession of goods changes, and in which the debtor–creditor relationship of the parties to the exchange was established, the possibility of default on the part of the purchaser being covered by the provision for doubtful debts, which effectively reduces the receivables figure in the balance sheet to net expected cash receipts. Especially where there is a substantial risk of default on the part of purchasers, however, it might be deemed imprudent to account the whole of the income from the transaction immediately on sale, and the second method defers the recognition of revenue until cash has been received, effectively spreading income over the credit period. Once again, neither method is theoretically objectionable, choice depending on the circumstances of the business, and in particular the kind of commodities sold and the financial reliability typical among its customers.

Discussion Topics

1. "The economic and legal requirements that the continuing lives of entities be divided into more or less arbitrary time periods create most of the measurement problems of accounting, and most of the need for an accounting theory." Discuss.

2. What are the difficulties associated with the measurement of income by the comparison of the net worth of an entity at the beginning and ending of an accounting period?

3. "Income receivable in the future is not as desirable (or valuable) as income receivable today. . . . " How, then, ought a loan of £5000 repayable 5 years hence to be shown in accounting statements?

4. "This is not to say that accounting measurements of income are 'true', but only that they are verifiable. . . . " If a measurement is verifiable, can it be other than true?

5. A "Transaction history" might be as short as a bus ride or as long as it takes to order, build and deliver a ship. How does the length of the "transaction history" affect the point at which costs and revenues are recognised in accounting?

6. How valid is "unexpired cost" as the basis for valuing long-term assets in period-end financial statements?

7. " . . . the not uncommon practice of treating all except long-term brand image advertising costs as period costs, expiring at the point of expenditure . . . is a distortion of the fundamental concept of matching costs against revenues." But what other procedure might be adopted?

8. Why is it "not possible . . . for an acceptable measure of past income and a statement of present worth of economic utility to be presented in a single series of articulated accounting statements. . . . "?

9. To what extent might "net income" be differently measured for

(a) reporting to shareholders,
(b) taxation purposes,
(c) appraisal of the performance of managers?

CHAPTER 8

Changing Money Values

THAT the value of money changes over periods of time is common knowledge. Every housewife knows it, though she would be likely to describe the phenomenon as "prices are always going up". Every wage-earner appreciates it, though the commonest interpretation is "having higher wages only to find they buy no more". Perhaps most acutely aware of the instability of money values are pensioners and others on fixed incomes. From them the cry arises "our incomes buy less and less".

At most times the purchasing power of money falls—inflation is the rule and not the exception. Sometimes, and in some conditions, inflation is rapid and on occasions has resulted in total loss of confidence in the currency unit. At other times, and elsewhere, inflation is hardly noticeable. But it is usually there. General deflation of prices and corresponding increase in money value are rare.

Nor is a continuing moderate degree of inflation necessarily undesirable. Rising prices of consumer goods encourage investment in productive equipment because of profit expectations, and this in turn stimulates employment and provides for higher incomes for wage-earners and profit sharers. Higher incomes create demand for consumer goods, and so the round begins again. Additionally, falls in the value of money lighten the burden of debt repayment. £10,000 borrowed 10 years ago and repayable now is still £10,000. But £10,000 now is not nearly so "big" a sum as it was then. As the value of money declines, the real cost of servicing debts becomes less.

Government policies with regard to inflation are not usually disposed to stop it, so much as to control it. An "inflationary spiral" is probably inevitable in an expanding economy pursuing a policy of full employment. The problem is to prevent its becoming too fast, to restrain money income growth to a level approximating to increases in productivity, and to keep the level of business activity in line with the supply of productive factors available.

Monetary Accounting, Inflation and the Profession

Accounting records are made in money terms. Assets and liabilities, income and expenditure are all accounted in money at prices ruling when transactions to buy or sell took place. Since the value of money is not constant, but usually falls over periods of time, accounting measurements of value, profit and loss, being measurements in purely monetary terms, by no means necessarily coincide with measures of purchasing power or economic surplus or deficit.

Accountants are, of course, not unaware of the impact on financial statements of changing money values but, no doubt conscious of the wide areas of discretion involved even in the construction of accounts on the basis of historic cost, some of which have been discussed in previous chapters, the official advice of the leading professional societies has in the past been against the general introduction of price-level adjustment accounting. The Institute of Chartered Accountants in England and Wales expressed its view as follows: [1]

"Unless and until a practicable and generally acceptable alternative is available, the Council recommends that the accounting principles set out below should continue to be applied:

(a) Historic cost should continue to be the basis on which annual accounts should be prepared and, in consequence, the basis on which profits shown by such accounts are computed.

[1] *Recommendations on Accounting Principles*, Recommendation 15, 1952, paras. 30 and 31.

(b) Any amount set aside out of profits in recognition of the effects which changes in the purchasing power of money have had on the affairs of the business (including any amount to finance the increase in the cost of replacements, whether of fixed or current assets) should be treated as a transfer to reserve and not as a charge in arriving at profits. If such a transfer is shown in the profit and loss account as a deduction in arriving at the balance for the year, that balance should be described appropriately, since it is not the whole of the profits.

(c) In order to emphasise that as a matter of prudence the amount so set aside is, for the time being, regarded by the directors as not available for distribution, it should normally be treated as a capital reserve.

(d) For balance sheet purposes fixed assets should not (except paragraph 12) be written-up, especially in the absence of monetary stability.

The Council also recommends to members who are directors or officers of companies or who are asked by their clients for advice, that they should stress the limitations on the significance of profits computed on the basis of historical costs in periods of material changes in the purchasing power of money; and that they should draw attention to the desirability of:

(a) Setting aside from profits to reserve in recognition of the effects which changes in the purchasing power of money have had upon the affairs of the business, particularly their effect on the amount of profit which, as a matter of policy, can prudently be regarded as available for distribution.

(b) Showing in the directors' report or otherwise the effects which changes in the purchasing power of money have had on the affairs of the business, including in particular the financial requirements for its maintenance and the directors' policy for meeting those requirements, either by setting aside to reserve or by raising fresh capital.

(c) Experimenting with methods of measuring the effects of changes in the purchasing power of money on profits and on financial requirements. If the results of such experiments are published as part of the documents accompanying the annual accounts, the basis used for the calculations and the significance of the figures in relation to the business concerned should be stated clearly."

The Institute's advice that "fixed assets should not be written up, especially in the absence of monetary stability" is a little curious, since in the *presence* of monetary stability there would be no occasion to make price-level adjustments to the stated values of assets. The recommendation advises the continuance of historic cost as the basis of profit computation, whilst admitting the "limitations on the significance of profits computed on [that] basis", and suggests that sums set aside in recognition of the effects of changes in the purchasing power of money should be treated as transfers to reserve made after the completion of the profit computation since "If such a transfer is shown in the profit and loss account . . . the balance for the year . . . is not the whole of the profits", but it does invite accountants to "experiment with methods of measuring the effects of changes in the purchasing power of money on profits and on financial requirements".

In the United States the American Institute of Certified Public Accountants took a view not dissimilar from that of the English Institute in stating: [1]

"Any basic change in the accounting treatment of depreciation should await further study of the nature and concept of business income.

The immediate problem can and should be met by financial management. The committee recognises that the common forms of financial statements may permit misunderstanding as to the amount which a corporation has available for distribution in the form of dividends, higher wages or lower prices for the company's products. When prices have risen appreciably since

[1] *Restatement and Revision of Accounting Research Bulletins,* 1953, p.69.

original investments in plant and facilities were made, a substantial proportion of net income as currently reported must be reinvested in the business in order to maintain assets at the same level of productivity at the end of the year as at the beginning.

Stockholders, employees, and the general public should be informed that a business must be able to retain out of profits amounts sufficient to replace productive facilities at current prices if it is to stay in business. The committee therefore gives its full support to the use of supplementary financial schedules, explanations or footnotes by which management may explain the need for retention of earnings."

The concern of both the English and the American Institutes as evidenced by their opinions quoted above was the retention within the business of funds adequate to maintain productive capacity in periods of rising prices, and it could well be that this objective can be achieved by "setting aside from profits to reserve in recognition of the effects which changes in the purchasing power of money have had on the affairs of the business . . . ", as the English Institute puts it, and that "The immediate problem can and should be met by financial management", as the American Institute says. Increased replacement costs are, however, only one aspect of the problem of changing money values. As long ago as 1952 a publication of the Taxation and Research Committee of the Association of Certified and Corporate Accountants pointed out: [1]

"From the economic point of view the essential feature of the [revaluation] technique that has been suggested in this present work is that it secures:
(a) *a proper computation of business income,* and
(b) a correct valuation of capital assets, by bringing all values into the same time dimension.

It allows an exact comparison of the *earning capacity* and indirectly of the efficiency of a given concern against others

[1] *Accounting for Inflation*, Gee & Co. Ltd., London, 1952.

in the same line of business through meaningful calculations of rates of profit against net worth." [Emphasis added.]

The stress here is not on the maintenance of productive capacity, but on the introduction of reporting methods superior to the questionable measurements of income based on *current* revenues and *historic* costs at present used. As the authors remarked:

" . . . the mere avoidance of possible distortion which the replacement cost technique allows, apart from any other advantages the technique might offer, would be sufficient reason for its adoption."

The basic argument for making adjustments for changing prices in accounting is to make the profit and loss account a more meaningful measure of the periodic income of an entity, and the balance sheet a more meaningful statement of its period-end financial position. The maintenance of productive capacity is another, though related, matter.

In 1958 the American Institute of Certified Public Accountants established the Accounting Principles Board and a Research Division. The Research Division conducts research into problems allocated for consideration to it by the Board, but the Division has authority to publish Accounting Research Studies without prior approval by the Institute or the Board as a stimulus to debate about possible improvements in accounting method. Three studies so far published have relevance, in varying degrees, to the problems of changing money values, and in each the emphasis is on the validity of accounting measurements. In *The Basic Postulates of Accounting* [1] Maurice Moonitz writes:

"The evidence of the instability of the monetary unit in recent decades is overwhelming; the probability that the instability will prevail into the foreseeable future is high . . . it is no longer realistic to ignore fluctuations in the value of the dollar."

and his postulate C-4 reads: "*Stable Unit*. Accounting reports should be based on a stable measuring unit."

[1] Accounting Research Study No. 1, A.I.C.P.A., New York, 1961.

Accounting Research Study No. 3, *A Tentative Set of Broad Accounting Principles for Business Enterprises* by Robert T. Sprouse and Maurice Moonitz [1] is closely integrated with Study No. 1, and carried the question of price-level changes in accounting further with comments such as:

"In the case of substantial monetary inflation appropriate conversion adjustments should be undertaken in order that the capital of the enterprise may be maintained in terms of the purchasing power invested by the stockholders", (p.72) and

"Fixed assets should be carried at cost of acquisition or construction, adjusted or converted when necessary to reflect substantial changes in purchasing power of the monetary unit" (p. 73).

Accounting Research Study No. 6, *Reporting the Effects of Price-Level Changes* [2] is wholly concerned with the subject of this chapter. It puts the objective clearly with the words (p.14):

" . . . if price-level changes can be measured in some satisfactory manner, and if the effects of those changes can be properly disclosed, the inferences that can be drawn from accounting data will be statistically more reliable. Specifically, for example, all the revenues and expenses in the earnings statement for any one year will be expressed in dollars of the same size and not in a mixture of dollars from different years. Similarly, the various balance-sheets will all be expressed in terms of a common dollar. Since both the results of operations and financial positions will be stated in terms of the same "common dollar", a calculation of a rate of return on invested capital can be made in which both numerator and denominator are expressed in the same units."

It should not be inferred that the publication of the Accounting Research Studies necessarily heralds the dawn of a new era of accounting. The studies are exploratory and speculative, and they deal with areas in which there is doubt and contention. There is, furthermore, the inherent conservatism of that part of the

[1] A.I.C.P.A., New York, 1962.
[2] A.I.C.P.A., New York, 1963.

profession in professional practice. Thus of Accounting Research Study No. 3 William W. Werntz wrote: (p.79 of the Study):

'I regret to have to say that I think it would be a disservice for this study to be published in its present form. . . . I am extremely fearful that, in the way in which the document has been prepared, there is an inadequate distinction between practices which have received general acceptance to date and those which you propose as additions or changes to existing practices."

Of Accounting Research Study No. 6, Robert C. Tyson wrote (p.252 of the Study):

"Although I have no aversion to the conduct of 'fundamental' research, I believe that research documents widely distributed to the members of the practising accounting profession and to industry should be directed toward 'applied' research. In other words, I feel that an academic approach, such as the subject study, will contribute toward a growing image of the profession as divided within itself with impractical and complex tendencies. Since I believe no amount of disclaimers can divorce research studies from the American Institute of Certified Public Accountants in the public mind, I do not recommend publication in its present form."

It being that Mr. Werntz and Mr. Tyson were members of the advisory committees associated with the studies (hence the publication of their comments in the reports), it would seem that the profession, though willing to encourage experiment, is still unready to change its official position on the question of price-level adjustment accounting.

Accounting in Current Prices: Long-term Assets

Because long-term assets are held for a number of accounting periods, and over a length of time in which price-levels might change considerably, they have been the focus of attention in the debate on revaluation, or constant-money accounting. Suppose a machine cost £100,000 and had a life of 5 years and no expected scrap value. The traditional accounting procedure would be to charge £20,000 to revenue in each year of the life of the asset, and to show its residual value in balance sheets at the ends of years 1 to 4 at £80,000, £60,000, £40,000 and £20,000 respectively. If the replacement price for the machine, or equipment of like utility to the entity, had risen to £150,000 by the end of year 5, £50,000 would have been transferred to capital reserve out of the profits of years 1 to 5 if the recommendations of the English Institute had been followed.

The main argument against this procedure is that it results in a distortion of the matching process—in the income statements for years 1 to 5 *current* revenues are matched against a *past* cost in calculating net income, and in the balance sheets presented at the ends of those years the asset would be shown at a largely meaningless figure, the "unexpired" historic cost. Furthermore, to follow the advice of the English Institute there would have to be profits of £50,000 available for transfer to capital reserve over the 5 years, and directors willing to make that transfer, and neither condition is certain to be satisfied. An alternative procedure suggested by advocates of revaluation accounting is to adjust the value of the asset at each period-end to its *replacement price*, and to revise depreciation charges so that in each period a segment of the replacement price, and not the historic cost is matched against revenue. If this were done, asset lists in balance sheets would be in terms of comparable, and current, money units, and net income would be the result of matching current revenues against current costs. The procedure used would be as follows:

Year ended 31 Dec.	Replacement cost (as shown in the balance sheet)	Depreciation charged against the revenue of the year
	£	£
1	110,000	22,000
2	120,000	24,000
3	130,000	26,000
4	140,000	28,000
5	150,000	30,000
		130,000

The accounting entries to achieve this result are, taking year 1 as an example:

Asset account	Dr	£10,000	
Capital revaluation reserve	Cr		£10,000
Profit and loss account	Dr	£22,000	
Provision for depreciation	Cr		£22,000

It might be noted that whilst the depreciation charge made in each year is the appropriate "matching" figure, one-fifth of the replacement or current cost of the asset in that year, the total depreciation charges do not add to the replacement cost of the machine. This is the result of not taking up as a charge to revenue in years 2 to 5 the shortfall of depreciation charges made in earlier years, as compared with current replacement costs in years 2 to 5, and it can be argued that the depreciation charge in year 2 (for example) should be £26,000, £24,000 being one-fifth of current replacement cost and £2000 being the shortfall in the depreciation charge made in year 1. There are two arguments against this procedure. The first is that it would distort the matching procedure in years 2 to 5. The charges made to income account in each of years 2 to 5 in the illustration were in each year the correct charges *having regard to the price level as it existed in each of those years,* and to make a further charge in respect of the *then correct* charges made in earlier years would result in an understatement of net income. The second is a rebuttal of the suggestion that the procedure advocated would accumulate something less than the replacement cost of the machine. Depreciation provisions do not lie idle, awaiting utilisation when replacement in fact falls due; they are employed immediately in the productive process of the business, and if the available funds were spent on assets, either long-term or working capital, subject to much the same price change influences as the asset in respect of which they were provided, their value would appreciate automatically over the life of the machine, generating total available funds approximate to replacement cost by the end of the machine's life. Put another way, to provide (e.g. in year 2) the extra £2000 for depreciation would be to provide for the price-level change *twice.* Thus, assuming that the depreciation provisions were invested in assets subject to a price-level increase of 10% per annum, the effect would be: [1]

Year	Aggregate depreciation provisions by 31 Dec. £	Increase in value of assets representing depreciation provisions £
1	22,000	
2	46,000	2200
3	72,000	4600
4	100,000	7200
5	130,000	10,000
		24,000

The aggregate depreciation provisions, plus the increase in "value" of the assets in which they were invested, approximates to the replacement cost of £150,000.

The increase in the balance sheet value of the asset has not affected the income measurement in any year, except to the extent that depreciation charges have been made in terms of current cost. The £50,000 increase in the replacement cost of the asset has been matched by the creation of a capital reserve of like amount; it has not been recognised as a profit, or even as a "holding gain"—the value of the asset and the owners' equity have merely been restated at the end of each accounting period as adjusted for changes in price-levels. Thus a comparison of the balance sheets shows:

Balance Sheet as at 1 Jan. 01

	£		£
Capital	100,000	Asset (at cost)	100,000

Balance Sheet as at 31 Dec. 05

	£		£
Capital	100,000	New asset (at cost)	150,000
Capital revaluation reserve	50,000		
	150,000		150,000

[1] The illustration has been simplified by using simple, and not compound interest, but it serves to illustrate the point.

The company is no better off at the end of year 5 than it was at the beginning of year 1, all that has happened is that, due to changes in price levels, the cost of the asset needed to continue the business has risen by 50% and this has been recognised by balance sheet adjustments.

Accounting in Current Prices: Inventories

The professional societies recommend that inventories should be valued for reporting purposes at the lower of cost or market value. The justification for this procedure is that, as a matter of prudence, losses should be recognised as soon as they are objectively evidenced, but that profits should not be accounted until they are realised at the point of sale, but as was demonstrated in Chapter 6, "cost" might mean any one of several things and, particularly in the case of work-in-progress, it might not be possible to establish "market value".

The advocates of accounting for changing prices attack the traditional procedure because the matching of *current* revenue from goods sold against costs of production incurred in *past* periods results in a distortion of net income and, in times of rising prices, an overstatement of profits. The last in, first out inventory pricing system is one approach to this problem, but it is by no means a satisfactory one in that even the most recently purchased items of stock might have been bought some time ago, when prices were different from current prices, and that when the most recently purchased stock is used up pricing reverts to earlier, and probably now quite irrelevant, purchase costs. Those who advocate the use of current market buying (replacement) prices argue that changes in the replacement prices of inventories occasion neither profits nor losses; they require a restatement equally of the carrying value of the stock and of the equity of the owners of the entity. The traditional and the current market buying price approaches might be compared:

Stock on hand on 1 January 02 1000 units purchased in year 1 at £3 each.

Sales in Year 2: 500 units at £5 each
Current market cost of stock on 31 December 02 £4 per unit.

Traditional Approach

Income Account for year ended 31 Dec. 02

	£
Sales (500 units at £5 each)	£2500
Less cost of sales (500 units at £3 each)	1500
Net income	1000

Balance Sheet as at 31 Dec. 02

	£		£
Capital	£1500	Inventories (500 units at £3 each)	£1500
Retained earnings	1000	Bank	1000
	£2500		£2500

A Current Market Buying Price Approach

Immediately it became known that the replacement cost of the stock had risen to £4, (and it is assumed that this was on 1 January 02) the inventory account is adjusted:

		£	£
Inventory account	Dr	£1000	
Capital revaluation reserve	Cr		£1000
(Recognition of a change in the cost price of 1000 units of stock from £3 to £4 per unit)			

and all stock issued to production or sold after that date would be at the newly established current cost of £4. The income statement and balance sheet published at the end of year 2 would be as follows:

Income Account for year ended 31 Dec. 02

	£
Sales (500 units at £5 each)	2500
Low cost of sales (500 units at £4 each)	2000
Net income	500

Balance Sheet as at 31 *Dec.* 02

	£		£
Capital	1500	Inventories (500 units at £4 each)	2000
Capital revaluation reserve	1000		
Retained earnings	500	Bank	1000
	3000		3000

Once again, the revision of the value of the asset *of itself* had no impact on the calculation of income, the recognition of the new price on 1 January 02 had the effect of increasing the inventory value and the owners' equity by the same amount; there had been no profit and no holding gain—the business was in no way better off in that there had been no change in its holdings of assets. Only when some of the stock was sold did a difference appear. The traditional approach matched current selling price of £5 against a past purchase price of £3, whilst the revaluation method matched current selling and buying prices, £5 and £4, hence the difference in reported net income.

Accounting for Changing Prices: Monetary Items

If cash of £1000 is held through a period when all prices rise by 10% (i.e. the purchasing power of money falls by 10%), the end-period £1000 has a purchasing power of only £900 in terms of pounds at the beginning of the period. Whilst physical assets held over a period of price-change automatically adjust in "value" (expressed in terms of money), monetary assets so held lose "value" (in terms of what money will buy). This is a *real* loss, a loss of the command over resources of the money held. Firms do not usually hold large sums of money, as such, over long periods of time, but the term "monetary items" embraces claims to cash as well as cash itself, e.g. loans either by or to the entity, and sundry debtors and sundry creditors. In price-level accounting the reality of changes in purchasing power on the value of monetary items is recognised in the income statement in the following manner: [1]

The average cash holding of an entity through a year was £1000.

The purchasing power of money fell by 10% over the accounting period.

> Profit and loss account   Dr   £100
> Capital revaluation reserve   Cr   £100
> (Recognition of the loss through the reduced purchasing power of average cash holdings, and maintenance of the purchasing power of invested capital.)

The Capital Revaluation Reserve

The Capital Revaluation Reserve is not the "sin bin" of revaluation accounting, a sort of repository for all unwanted debits and credits. It has two important purposes. The first of these is the collection in one account of all the effects of price-level changes on all the entity's assets and liabilities in each accounting period, and the second is that read in conjunction with the shareholders' (or other owners') capital account, the capital revaluation reserve reflects the present purchasing power of the assets constituting the owners' investment. Thus, summing up the transactions shown in the illustrations in the three preceding sections, the capital revaluation reserve account would appear as follows:

Capital Revaluation Reserve Account for year ended 31 *Dec.* 02

	£		£
Income account (page 125)	100	Long-term asset account (page 119)	20,000
		Inventory account (page 123)	1000

[1] Note that this procedure is applicable only to cash or claims to fixed amounts of future cash. Equity holdings in other entities (e.g. ordinary shares) should be shown at market value—they are not claims on future money but on the assets of other entities, and should be treated in price-change accounting as non-monetary, long-term assets.

and in the balance sheet it would be shown:

Balance Sheet as at 31 *Dec.* 02

	£	£
Owners' equity		
Capital	100,000	
Capital revaluation reserve	20,900	120,900

Current Market Buying Prices and Index Numbers

In the discussion thus far it has been assumed that the current market buying (replacement) prices of assets can readily be determined. Such is sometimes the case: market prices of raw materials are usually known, and it is sometimes possible to discover an ex-factory price for partly finished and finished goods. Commonly, however, the replacement price of an asset cannot be determined because there is no market in which exchange transactions are taking place. This is often true of work-in-progress, and of long-term assets. In such cases revaluation is effected by the use of specific price indexes.

An entirely different approach is to apply a single index of price changes to *all* assets and liabilities, with the objective of estimating the overall effect on the business of changes in the purchasing power of money. Those who adopt this approach desire to restate the *investment in assets* (and not the assets themselves) in accordance with movements in the value of money *per se*. This approach is supported by Accounting Research Study 6, p.xi:

"Restatement by means of a single index of the general price level is not a means of introducing replacement costs into the financial statements. To introduce replacement costs requires the use of current market prices, or appraisals, or a series of highly specific indexes, one for each account or group of accounts in the financial statements. For the sake of simplicity and precision in analysis, this study assumes that replacement costs are *not* to be introduced into the financial statements. With or without replacement costs, the measurement and disclosure of the effects of changes in the purchasing power of the dollar (as measured by an index of the movement of *all* prices) is still desirable."

This is a simple solution to the problem, and because only one index is applied to all values, it reduces the amount of subjective judgement required of the accountant and renders his calculations easily capable of independent verification. The single index system is favoured by those who emphasise the impact of changes in price-levels on the shareholders' equity; in converting all values on the basis of a purchasing-power index, the capital revaluation reserve becomes specifically a recognition of changes in the value of the original capital investment. R. S. Gynther says of the single index school: [1]

"One school advocates the using of one general index for all necessary adjustments of expenses, and its members want this index to represent the movement in the prices of all the goods and services in the country. They want the index to represent the movements in the prices of 'all things in general'. They want the index to be the reciprocal of the value of money itself. They want their index to measure pure inflation or deflation—as distinct from movements in the prices of specific items or groups of items. This school wants to adhere closely to the concept of historical cost in that they merely wish to restate all past costs in accordance with the current value of the currency unit.

If it is felt that the whole purpose of accounting is to look after the interests of the shareholders or proprietors, then it is almost certain that the use of one general index will be favoured for profit determination purposes; so that the number of purchasing-power units contained in the monies subscribed to the business by shareholders will be maintained throughout a period of changing prices."

[1] R. S. Gynther, *Accounting for Price-level Changes—Theory and Procedures,* Pergamon Press Ltd., Oxford, 1966, pp. 41 *et seq.*

The alternative approach stresses changes in the values of specific assets or groups of assets and liabilities within the entity. It involves the use of actual replacement prices where they are known, and indexes specific to particular kinds of assets where replacement prices are not known. The emphasis is not on the changing purchasing power of the equity investment, but on the changing values of the assets and liabilities of the entity when there are price-level changes. Of this approach Professor Gynther says: [1]

"The other school advocates the using of several specific indexes, with each index measuring the specific movement in the relative expense for the firm. They wish to restate the historical cost of each item in accordance with the specific cost of that item. They want to record the effect of price-level changes as they affect each specific firm. They do not want to record the effect of the general inflation or deflation, which by itself is considered to be irrelevant. They claim that the movements in the 'prices of all things in general' have no specific bearing on each individual or individual firm. They claim that it is only the movements in prices of those things in which each firm or individual is interested that are relevant, in each case.

. . . if it is believed that the whole or prime purpose of accounting is to assist the entity (the firm) in its daily struggles (and that only in this way will the interests of shareholders be looked after in the long term), then it is almost certain that the use of specific indexes will be favoured, i.e. so that the physical assets of the business will be maintained during the period of changing prices."

The two approaches are not merely marginally different ways of looking at the same thing, nor even different technical ways of tackling the same job; they are wholly different in concept,

[1] *op. cit.,* pp. 42 *et seq.*

different in their view of what accounting is *about*. Professor Gynther stresses the point: [1]

"It seems that those who look upon a company from outside its four walls will want its profit determined with the aid of one general index. . . . Their prime interest is that of the share-holders (consciously or subconsciously)."

"It seems, too, that those who look upon a company as from within will want its profit determined with the aid of specific indexes (or specific prices if available). People in this category often feel as if they are part of the firm. . . . Their prime interest is that of the company itself."

Integrated Accounting or Supplementary Reports

The cautious advice of the English Institute on experimentation with price-change accounting, given in 1952, clearly had in mind (see p. 114) that any price-level adjusted figures should be merely supplementary to traditionally based financial reports, and that "the basis used for the calculations and the significance of the figures in relation to the business concerned should be clearly stated". Attitudes have changed little among the professional societies since, then: in 1963 Accounting Research Study No. 6 declared (p.xi):

"The effects of price-level changes should be disclosed as a supplement to the conventional statements. This disclosure may take the form of physically separate statements, or of parallel columns in a combined statement, or of detailed supporting schedules (including charts and graphs), or some combination of these."

Professional societies, in their pronouncements, usually have as their *primary* concern, the published financial reports of corporations, and they are ever mindful, and rightly so, of the difficult task of the auditor who has to express an opinion on

[1] *op. cit.*, pp. 45 and 46.

published accounts. The great majority of accounting reports, however, are neither published nor audited—they are used by managers and directors in the conduct of the continuing business of their enterprises. As Professor A. Goudeket remarks: [1]

> "The object of the accounting system is to provide the management of each section of the concern with the information it requires for operating that particular section, and to provide the top management of the concern with the information required for its central management.
>
> In accordance with the principles of 'accounting for management' the responsible managers of all levels must know periodically the income and the capital employed, both in total and in detail. For this purpose the replacement value (i.e. *current* replacement value) is applied. In other words, the application of the replacement value theory is not merely a calculation technique used in preparing the annual statements of the concern. It is integrated in the accounting system of all sections of the concern at every stage. In this way it is ensured that all information for management is compiled in accordance with this principle and thus the replacement value automatically enters into all management considerations and decisions."

Here again we are confronted with a difference of opinion more fundamental that the substance of the debate, with the basic question of what accounting is *for*, and for whose benefit accounting is *primarily* done. If the end-product of the accounting system, the published financial reports, are accorded primary importance, the logical conclusion is that information on price-level changes should be given in supporting schedules, or in some other way along with the traditional income statement and balance sheet. Shareholders and others using the accounts would have at their disposal additional information about changes in the purchasing power of the equity of the entity, without being deprived of the traditional statements they are accustomed to receive. If, on the

[1] *Journal of Accountancy*, July 1960, p.38. Professor Goudeket was Chief Internal Auditor of Philips Electrical Industries.

other hand, recording and reporting on internal flows of value are considered to be the major objectives of accounting, the whole of the system would be subject to continuous price-level adjustment, and the extraction from the records of traditional (historic cost) period-end statements would be a difficult task.

There is no doubt about the practicability of accounting for changes in price levels—Philips Electrical Industries have operated a comprehensive system for many years, and partial value adjustments, usually of long-term assets, are made periodically by many companies. What is in doubt is whether accounting for price-level changes is desirable, and, if it is, which revaluation and reporting techniques are the most appropriate. It is easy to point to the fallacies inherent in accounting on a basis of historic costs, but it is equally easy to demonstrate that revaluation accounting opens up large areas of subjectivity in accounting measurement. The continuing debate on price-level changes, and their effect on accounting reports, seems unlikely to be terminated until there emerges a group of principles capable of being generally accepted.

Discussion Topics

1. Why is inflation of prices the rule, rather than the exception, and why is this not undesirable?

2. Is it still true to say, as the A.I.C.P.A. did in 1953, that: "Any basic change in the accounting treatment of depreciation should await further study of the nature and concept of business income."?

3. Why might William W. Werntz and Robert C. Tyson have advised against the publication of Accounting Research Studies Nos. 3 and 6 "in their present form"?

4. What should be the basis for depreciation charges under a system of revaluation accounting?

5. What are the objectives of the capital revaluation account?

6. "Single index revaluation and multiple index revaluation is not a choice of technique, it is a difference of philosophy." Discuss.

7. "The decision as to whether price-level changes shall be continuously integrated into the accounting records as they occur, or whether price-level changes should be reported as a supplement to traditional-period-end financial statements is a decision about the basic objective of accounting." Discuss.

8. "It is better to be vaguely right than precisely wrong" (attributed to J. M. Keynes). Is this true of financial reporting?

CHAPTER 9

Towards a Theory of Business Accounting *

LIKE all invented devices, accounting must be supposed to be of use to some persons or classes of persons. However well or poorly it might be done it must serve some function. If the function can be ascertained and specified, it will be possible to deduce the form which accounting should take. And if the ideal form of accounting can be stated it should be possible to judge whether or not any present practice yields information which will serve the stipulated function and in what direction improvements may be made. This is the aim of theorising. In what follows, therefore, no attempt is made to describe what practitioners do. Rather an attempt is made to draw from the environment of accounting some generalisations about its necessary characteristics which will be of wide application.

The act of accounting has an economic setting. It is expected to add to the knowledge of those who engage in commercial and financial interaction. To construct some general notions about accounting, it is therefore necessary to draw on knowledge of the ways in which people act, individually and collectively, in economic matters. As social behaviour, including economic behaviour, is regulated by laws and customs having the same effects as laws, it is necessary to draw on knowledge of the legal and conventional framework. And as accounting is a

*By R. J. Chambers. This is a simplified and modified version of a paper Towards a General Theory of Accounting, first written in 1961. The basic ideas are unchanged, but the conclusions differ in some important respects. The necessity for these changes became apparent when writing *Accounting, Evaluation and Economic Behaviour*, completed in December 1964, and on subsequent reflection. The present form represents the author's view as at the end of 1968.

process by which selected information is processed and communicated, its study must draw on parts of the field of the communication sciences, such as the use of verbal and numerical symbols.

Out of this mixture of psychological, economic, legal and other notions must be spun a coherent network of propositions which will serve as a basis for an ideal accounting.

Individuals as Actors

The human individual is a complex organism, having basic needs, capable of having wants other than basic needs, and capable of perception, reflection, imagination and action. His basic needs and other wants and the influence of his environment contrive to establish in him a set of bodily and mental conditions, his actual state at any point of time. If he imagines a preferred state which differs from his actual state at a point of time, he has an incentive to act, to relieve the strain due to the difference between actual and preferred states. If he imagines a number of preferred states he must choose between them. He must rank them, for at any time he cannot take more than a limited number of steps to secure his varied wants. He will value most highly that course of action which he expects will satisfy his wants at the time to the greatest possible extent.

But wants change from time to time. So, therefore, will preferences change. Notice, however, that the incentive to act arises from the difference between an actual, discovered state and a preferred, imagined state. It follows that any thought about acting requires the present state to be known. Further, if a person wishes to think of acting in some way other than the way he has acted in the past, it is useful to have knowledge of the consequences of acting as he did it in the past. With this knowledge he may the better imagine what may happen by proceeding similarly in the future, even though he has to construct in imagination the possible consequences of different actions without corresponding knowledge of the past.

Means

Every action requires the appropriation or sacrifice of means. Means are all things believed to be serviceable in satisfying wants. Means include labour, natural things, artifacts and rights. The means available to any person are limited. Indeed, the means available to any community of persons are scarce relatively to their wants. There are consequently property and other laws which secure the rights in means to particular persons, and reduce the possibility of conflict over possession among the members of the community.

Some means serve only specific wants; others may serve many different wants. Some means are more durable than others. Some are larger in unit size than others. Some are scarcer than others. These diverse characteristics entail that different means will be wanted by different persons at varying times for varying purposes, and that the want of any person for any means will be of varying intensity. That means which a person wants more intensely than other means is said to have the greatest utility for him in the state of his wants at that time. The utility of any means is not, therefore, a property of that means but a feature of the attitude of a person towards it. As persons ordinarily want means specific to various kinds of satisfaction, the more one has of a specific means the less one is willing to sacrifice to obtain an addition to that quantity. This principle of diminishing marginal utility helps to explain the changes in preferences men may have. But it is only a partial explanation of the prices asked and paid for means.

The Environment

The environment is the complex of natural and constructed things, persons, laws, customs and other devices, and events which surround and impinge on an individual person. It determines, in part, the state in which he finds himself at any time. It causes some of the strains he feels and provides some of the opportunities for the relief of strain. Laws and customs and the durability of goods and the persistence of habits make the future environment predictable to some degree. But in many respects the environment is fluid and unpredictable. Consequently when an actor imagines or calculates the outcome of a course of action, he cannot be sure that it will turn out as he expected.

The uncertainty of the future makes actions taken in expectation of distant effects more or less risky. And some kinds of actions are by their nature more risky than others. One expects the payoff of any particular risky action to be greater than the payoff of a riskless action, to compensate for the possibility that the payoffs of some risky actions will be less than expected. Assessments of risk are personal. Like other assessments of means in relation to wants they enter into the determination of utility.

The characteristic economic activities of men are production, exchange and consumption. Production is the combination of means for the creation of things which are more serviceable in relation to wants than the original means themselves. Consumption is the appropriation of means for the satisfaction of immediate wants. The difference between production and consumption is saving. Saving is the provision of means for the service of future wants. It depends on there being some durable means.

The use of means in production and their exchange and consumption require that individuals or associations of individuals shall have the right to hold and dispose of means. These rights are secured by the framework of laws and customs which define ownership, possessory and user rights. Given such laws, any individual can be said to stand in a certain relationship to the rest of the community and its members in respect of means.

The individual members of a society have different skills and capacities. A society tends to arrange its productive processes so that, by taking advantage of the special contributions of individuals, the wants of its members might be satisfied to a greater extent than would be possible if individuals were to act in isolation. The link between such specialised styles of production and the satisfaction of consumption is exchange.

Action in a Market Economy

Exchanges may be immediate, some goods for others, some services for others, at the same time. Or a transferor may part with possession on the understanding that the transferee will perform his part of a bargain at a future date. Such transfers are credit transactions. Though the transferor trusts that the transferee will perform his part, he has assurance of this by the availability of legal remedies against non-performance.

Most exchanges are indirect, mediated by the use of money or of records of debts and claims expressed in terms of money units. Without the use of money, exchanges would be possible only if both parties had goods or services which were acceptable to each other as fair exchanges. But differences in the size, scarcity and utility of means make such occurrences rare. The use of money greatly increases the possibility of exchange. In a money economy, the general acceptance of money as a medium of exchange provides a convenient way of expressing the ratio at which goods and services are exchanged for other goods and services. The ratio is a price—so many monetary units for such and such a good.

For individuals, money is a means like other means. But its utility is indirect. It enables its possessor to acquire other things which serve wants. It has been noted that wants may change and rankings of things preferred may change. There is a risk in holding goods, therefore, that the holder may want them less intensely than other goods at some time, and may have to sell them to acquire the other goods. It is much less inconvenient to hold money which can be laid out for whatever goods one wants from time to time.

But there are risks in holding money too. It is well known that a given number of units of money will not buy the same quantity of things at one time as at another. If the prices of many things rise and the prices of few fall, we speak of a fall in the purchasing power of money. Men will then want more units of money than before to obtain the same relief from wants as before. Men want money for its purchasing power only.

At any point of time men having money and wanting goods do not worry about the purchasing power of money. They are confronted with the prices of the various things they can buy and will simply choose to buy the goods which seem to them to be preferable to others, given the prices they have to pay. But whenever it is necessary to compare or relate particular prices or money sums for the purpose of reflecting on past or future action, it is necessary to take account of the differences, if any, in the purchasing power of the monetary units at the several points of time in question. Account is taken of these differences by the use of an index of the general purchasing power of money.

The prices of goods, their ratios of exchange for money, are determined in markets. That means have utility explains why they are wanted. But it is the supply of them and the demand for them which determines their prices and changes in those prices. Prices are not measures of the utility of goods to buyer or seller. A price paid is simply the amount of money a buyer was willing to sacrifice to obtain the good. As most goods and services may be bought and sold at a price stated in money units, and as the possession of money or of goods which can be sold for money generally limits what one can buy, all reckoning about the purchase and sale of goods is done in monetary units.

Financial Position

Because money and debts and claims expressed in monetary units are so widely used, individuals and associations of individuals find it useful to keep account of the money they hold and the monetary equivalents (prices) of the non-monetary goods and rights they possess and the money they owe to others. Separate accounts may be kept of all of these things. As money is wanted to buy goods and services and to pay debts, the relevant prices of the non-monetary goods and rights they hold are resale prices. But not because they intend to resell; only because the resale price can be added to the cash in hand and claims against others (if any) to give the total amount of money which could be available to buy other things or to pay debts owed. We will call the money amounts for the several classes of assets, as described in the last sentence, their current cash equivalents.

The rights of a person in means were said above to constitute the relationship of a person to the rest of a community in respect of means. Means in which a person has rights of possession at a given time are described as his assets. Amounts of money he owes to others at a given time are described as his liabilities; the liabilities of one person may also be described as equities of others in his assets, for they have a right to be paid out of his assets. The difference between his rights of possession against the rest of the community and the rights of other members of the community to be paid out of his assets is his net ownership of rights against the rest of the community, or his residual equity in means possessed. If the assets and their current cash equivalents are stated and the amounts of the equities of others and of the person himself are stated, both at a given point of time, we may describe the whole statement as a statement of the financial position of the person at that time, his financial position in relation to the rest of the community. Clearly, by the manner of definition the sum of the measures of assets is equal to the sum of the measures of equities. A statement of this kind is described as a balance sheet for it summarises the corrected balances of the asset and equity accounts at the date it bears.

If a man knows his financial position he may deduce the difference between it and some preferred position. He will know the amounts and the composition of assets with which he may try to reach the preferred position. He will be able to think about the various ways by which he can reach that position. He will know the constraints which his liabilities impose on those ways.

Individuals commonly have limited ways of varying their salary or wage incomes by their own actions. Business firms, however, may vary their operations in many ways to increase their incomes. We will therefore use as illustration of income calculation a simple business firm, though what we have already said applies to firms and what we shall say hereafter applies generally to persons.

Business Firms

Firms which are companies have most of the same legal rights and may have most of the same property relations as have individuals. Firms which are not companies are deemed to have the same rights, even though the satisfaction of claims against them lies strictly against their owners as individuals.

Firms buy and sell goods and services in the expectation of profits or business income. They carry stocks of goods and invest in durable equipment with this object. They change their holdings of goods and equipment as shifts in the expectation of profit are induced by shifts in the demand for products or in the conditions of supply of the goods and services they use. As the range of products sold, the prices at which they are sold, the range of services used and the prices of those services may all change or be changed from time to time, there can be no assurance that an expected profit will in fact arise. It is necessary therefore to have an account of the profits earned periodically to discover what profit has arisen and to consider in what ways, if any, the general policies or specific decisions of the firm should be varied.

A business firm obtains money in the first place from one or more investors. The firm is managed by a manager who is held accountable by the investors both for the money originally contributed and the money and other assets subsequently acquired, and for the effectiveness with which the assets are used. Because means are scarce relative to wants, an investor will seek to invest in the firm or firms which he expects will bring him the greatest gain. The effectiveness with which assets are used is a guide to this. It is given by the rate at which the residual equity is increased in a given period. Because business income may be compared, by investors and managers, with income from other forms of investment on which annual interest or rents are paid, the basic period for calculations is the year. The annual change in the residual equity is the annual profit; and the test of effectiveness is the rate of return, the percentage relationship of profit to residual equity.

The annual profit of a business is not necessarily the annual income of investors in it, for part of the profit may be retained to build up the business in the expectation of greater future profits. If the rate of return justifies this expectation the share of an investor in a business may be able to be sold at a profit to the investor. If the rate of return does not compare favourably with other investment opportunities, the possibility of selling the business and investing the proceeds otherwise may be considered. Clearly the rate of return is used in a variety of ways by managers and investors.

Income Calculation

The profit of a business may be ascertained in two ways. The difference between the measures of the residual equity at the beginning and end of the year may be taken. Or one may accumulate the revenues and other gains and the expenses and other losses, and take the difference. Both ways should yield the same answer. As managers may wish, during a year, to see what progress they are making towards a year's expected profit and whether the combination of business assets is still satisfactory, a continuous record is kept so that more or less up-to-date information is available at any time.

The difference between the measures of residual equity at the opening and closing dates of a period will be the amount of the profit of the firm, if there has been no net change in the purchasing power of money in the period. To take this difference is mathematically correct, for the two measures are in units having the same significance. But if there has been a change in the purchasing power of money, it is not correct mathematically to deduct a sum which represents purchasing power at one date from a sum which represents purchasing power at another. The units are not the same in significance. In any case, we are not better off at one date than at another if we simply have more money tokens but they will buy no more than before. Profit is meaningless unless we are better off, whether "we" are persons or business firms.

If the purchasing power of money has changed we must convert the opening measure of net assets (which is equal to the measure of residual equity) to the appropriate number of monetary units of the purchasing power at the close of the period. We may then subtract this from the measure of net assets at the close of the period to obtain the profit of the year in terms of units of purchasing power at the close of the period. The amount of the adjustment to the opening measure of net assets is simply due to the change in the significance of the measuring unit between the two dates; it should be shown in the statement of financial position at the end of the period separately from the profit earned. It may be called a capital maintenance adjustment.

Formal Demonstration

The system described may be represented briefly as follows.

Let $\$_1$ and $\$_2$ represent dollars of the purchasing power prevailing at dates t_1 and t_2, the opening and closing dates of a period.

Let $\$_1 M_1$ and $\$_2 M_2$ be the measures of net monetary assets at the two dates. Net monetary assets are cash and receivables less payables.

Let $\$_1 N_1$ and $\$_2 N_2$ be the measures of non-monetary assets at the two dates, that is to say the sums of the resale prices of assets other than monetary assets.

Let $\$_1 R_1$ and $\$_2 R_2$ be the measures of the residual equity at the two dates.

Now at t_1

$$\$_1 M_1 + \$_1 N_1 = \$_1 R_1,$$

and at t_2

$$\$_2 M_2 + \$_2 N_2 = \$_2 R_2.$$

The left-hand sides of these equations are true and complete, for they are derived by observation of the assets in possession and the resale prices of non-monetary assets. We wish to interpret the right-hand sides in such a way as to give the profit for the year.

Let the proportionate change in the purchasing power of the dollar be p (expressed as a decimal fraction), so that $\$_1 = \$_2(1+p)$. The residual equity at t_1 may therefore be represented by $\$_2(1+p)R_1$. The difference between the residual equities at t_2 and t_1 is then $\$_2(R_2-R_1-R_1 p)$ and the amount of the residual equity at t_2 may be shown as:

Opening residual equity	R_1
Capital maintenance adjustment	$R_1 p$
Profit of year	$(R_2-R_1-R_1 p)$
Closing residual equity	$\$_2 R_2$

It matters not how many transactions and events during the year have given rise to the change from the magnitude R_1 to the magnitude R_2. The events and transactions giving rise to changes in all assets and liabilities may have been accumulated in accounts of revenues and expenses and other accounts so that the number R_1 accumulates to the number R_2. There may be difficulties in determining some of the magnitudes, so that the magnitudes shown for assets, and the derived figures for residual equity, may simply be the best possible approximations. But given a solution to these difficulties the above adjustment is the only further step necessary.

Although in the above demonstration the signs $\$_1$ and $\$_2$ have been used, the only sign used in ordinary commerce is $\$$. But the mere fact that a balance sheet bears a date signifies that the statements it contains are statements made at that date, and interpretable at that date by reference to prices then ruling. At that date the prices of prior dates are of historical interest only and are of no consequence in relation to any contemplated ransaction.

Summary

1. Accounting deals with quantities of money, the money prices of non-monetary goods, and the monetary amounts of rights and claims. The particular and aggregated statements it yields contain information necessary in judging the consequences of past events and in forming plans and expectations about future courses of action.

2. Any such set of statements relates to a specific entity, among the characteristics of which is the power or right to enter into contracts and exchanges with other entities in the community at large.

3. The financial position of an entity is the financial relationship in which it stands to the rest of the community at a point of time. A statement of financial position will consist of a statement of assets, including non-monetary assets at resale prices, and of the equities of creditors and of the residual interest in those assets. The aggregates of the monetary equivalents of assets and equities will be equal.

4. The income of an entity for a period is the difference in the amounts of the net assets (or residual equity) at the beginning and end of the period, provided the purchasing power of the monetary unit remains unchanged. If the purchasing power of the monetary (measuring) unit changes during a period, allowance must be made for the change in calculating income.

5. The financial position and the income (or profit) of an entity are represented at the end of any given period in monetary units of contemporary purchasing power. They are interpretable at that time by any person in the light of prevailing prices.

6. The information conveyed by statements of financial position and income is relevant, as factual information at the time, to all classes of person associated with an entity, whether as owner, manager or financier.

7. If the information is compiled or prepared by any specialist, no rule or guide should be adopted by the specialist which interferes with the best possible approximation to the position and income as described above.

8. If rules which are similar in effect are adopted by all firms, comparisons may be made between firms for the purpose of assessing relative performances as a guide to future action.

9. There may be difficulties in determining some of the resale prices of assets, and hence in determining some of the costs of a period. But as the object of presenting information is to enable readers to reflect upon the past and upon the future possibilities, no damage will arise if those amounts are approximate provided they are of the correct order of magnitude.

PART III ENVIRONMENT

CHAPTER 10

Economics and Accounting

THOUGH modern economists have become increasingly concerned with problems of growth, employment and price policy, much of economics remains as it has traditionally been defined: the study of the allocation of scarce means among competing uses to obtain optimum results. It is beyond question that means are limited. Known physical resources are limited. There is a limited quantity of manpower. There is a limited amount of productive equipment of all kinds. Time is limited, and, not least, technical ability is limited. Though there are wealthy people and wealthy nations, there are none whose condition could not be improved, were more means available. There are people and nations whose means are so limited that they exist on the barest essentials of life.

Nor can it be disputed that there are unlimited uses to which the scarce means could be put, and that these uses compete one with another. A wealthy man might be able to afford to own two cars or a bigger house or to take an overseas holiday, but might not be able to do more than one of these. For a poor man the choice might be between feeding his family, warming his house or getting drunk. One, but not the others; or maybe part of one, and part of the others. A wealthy nation might be able to choose between the status of a thermo-nuclear power and social benefits for its citizens, but might not be able to achieve both. For a poor nation the choice might lie between providing improved levels of subsistence for its population, and diverting economic resources to basic programmes of industrialisation or education.

For all, rich and poor, individuals and nations alike, means are limited and ends are limitless and competing.

The procedures by which individuals and business and political groups seek to maximise the benefit they receive from their limited resources, the production of goods and services, the organisation of markets, the determination of prices and the creation and use of capital resources are the subject material of economics. These, however, are the substance not only of economics, but also of accounting. It is mainly to provide records of economic phenomena that accounting exists: if men did not engage in economic activity there would be nothing to account for. In a sense, whilst economics seeks to explain economic behaviour, accounting exists to record economic events and to provide a basis for economic policy.

Economic Change and the Development of Accounting

The nature of accounting is largely determined by its economic environment. Thus accounting services in feudal Europe were limited to the preparation of lists of rent payments due from the tenant to his lord, and statements regulating the allocation of land and the lord's claim on his tenant's labour. The manorial economy called forth no more than manorial accounting. Double-entry was the product of economic growth in fifteenth-century Italy, when extensive trading and manufacturing activities demanded an effective recording system. The continuing process of the Industrial Revolution further illustrates the point. The early factory accounts were not a chance invention, but an economic necessity, and their development into the complex range of modern management accounting techniques has done no more than keep pace with economic demand. The growth of the accountancy profession has not been accidental, but the product of economic pressures: the broadening base of industrial investment and the development of sophisticated systems of finance for industry and commerce, among other factors.

It might be noted that, whilst developments in accounting method have usually been prompted by economic change, this has not necessarily been economic expansion. Many of the refinements of cost accounting have their origin in wartime controls and cost reduction schemes introduced during times of economic depression, and practising accountants have derived not a little of their business from bankruptcies, insolvencies and company failures.

If economics and accountancy are so closely related, it might be expected that accountants and economists would be intimately associated in dealing with the economic problems of society. Accountants are recording information about the events economists seek to explain. They create a wealth of records on which economists might base their studies. On the other hand, if accounting records are to be of value, they must accord with economic realities: reports on business situations are only useful if they have been drawn in appreciation of the economic context of the firm. Such a close relationship between economists and accountants does not, however, exist. For several reasons.

Scale of Operations

A fundamental difference between economists and accountants is that economists are frequently interested in the affairs of nations, industries or whole markets, whilst accountants are more usually concerned in the affairs of single firms. Whilst both are analysing economic events, they are working on different scales of magnitude. Economists are generally disposed to consider large matters of policy in business affairs. Accountants are more usually engaged in professional work with the productive or exchange units which collectively constitute the economists' industry or market.

It is usually the case that, in considering large-scale problems, economists have available relevant accounting reports, but because those reports have not been constructed in accord with any generally accepted theory, but each on an individual firm's interpretation of accounting concepts, it is seldom possible for the economist to extract a useful aggregation. For example, an economist might be concerned to discover the value of raw material stocks in an industry. In accounting reports the stocks are shown as being valued on differing bases, such as "at cost or below" or "at cost or market value, whichever is lower". Aggregation of such figures would amount to no more than a summation of varied conservative opinions based on diverse lines of reasoning, each special to the firm whence it came and the accountant responsible for it.

There is a so-far unbridged gap between those economists interested in macro-economic analysis and accountants concerned with the everyday affairs of business and government, and this is to be regretted. The accounting reports of leading industrial and financial corporations are important economic records, and have economic consequences. Accounting calculations of profit and loss and statements of the financial positions of major concerns influence dividend policy, have their effect on the valuation of shares and provide indications of the progress and position, both of specific industries and of the economy at large. Whilst accounting is the main public reporting method of limited companies occupying a dominant position in the economy, economists of all kinds are ill equipped if they are unable to interpret and evaluate accounting statements.

Economists and the Theory of the Firm

In recent years greater interest has been shown by economists in units smaller than the nation or the industry. More attention has been directed towards understanding the aims and policies of individual business units. For this development there have been two main reasons. First, the wartime association of economists with the practical problems of production has carried over into the post-war period, and many firms retain the services of economists to assist in directing business policy. Second, new techniques in economic analysis, and in particular in economic statistics, having special relevance to business decision formation have been developed. In this area accountants and economists have been brought into close contact. The differences in their approaches to business problems have been thrown into sharp relief.

An assumption of many formal models of economic theory with regard to the individual firm is that it will so organise the means at its disposal and its processes of production as to maximise its profits. The economist is not, therefore, greatly concerned with past events as facts, except to the extent that he might analyse policies pursued for comparison with alternative policies not pursued. On looking at future policy, "bygones are bygones" for the economist: all that is relevant is that a variety of possible business ends might be achieved by the use of the resources at the disposal of the firm. The problem is to select that course of action which will result in the highest profit.

The chief weakness in this approach (and it is a weakness generally recognised among economists) is that firms by no means always have as their objective the maximisation of profits. Monopolists might limit their profits for fear of restrictive legislation; firms might prefer to carry on, though earning low profits, rather than wind up for a greater net return; directors might be more interested in power than profit; and firms might devote resources to the welfare of their workers for social, rather than economic, reasons. Nor has a business, in the pursuit of profit, unlicensed access to the world of commerce. The law of the jungle does not apply in the commercial affairs of even the most "private enterprise" state. Legal and conventional restraints on business activity are many and varied, and might preclude otherwise attractive lines of policy.

Though the more simple models used in the theory of the firm have an attractive mathematical symmetry, theoretical models are seldom applicable to actual situations without extensive modification. Modern economists have become less concerned with abstract models as they have become more involved in the analysis of the structure of markets as they in fact are, and in dealing with problems of firms, industries and government agencies. They have sought to develop other tools of analysis, such as linear programming, to help in making decisions about the best allocation of resources.

In dealing with individual firms, whether preparing case studies for subsequent academic analysis, or for the purpose of giving advice on specific business problems, the economist is compelled to rely to a great extent on data supplied by the firm's accounting department. Inability by an economist to understand accounting method might result in accounts being ignored, or given undue emphasis, or being misinterpreted. Awakening of interest in accounting among economists has been a matter of necessity for those concerned with small-scale economic units.

The Accountant and the Firm

Two things have distinguished the typical approaches of economists and accountants to business problems. The first is that accountants have traditionally been economic historians—their first interest is in calculating the profits or losses of enterprises for past periods and in stating financial positions at past points in time. This is the inevitable product of professional practice. Profits must be calculated so that dividends might be declared or drawings justified, and period-end financial statements are statutory reports of stewardship by directors to their shareholders.

Secondly, accountants are more likely than economists to be aware of the legal and conventional restraints on business policy. Once again, this is a product of professional practice in finance. Considerations of company law, taxation, labour agreements and trade regulations are relevant to decision making, and they are the stock-in-trade of accountancy. Accountants are not infrequently accused of becoming so involved in environmental restraints on business policy that they lose perspective; coming to regard the firm not as a dynamic profit-making venture, but as a creature of statute and convention, responsive mainly to external restraints and stimuli.

For several reasons accountants are reorienting their approach to business problems, and giving closer attention to matters of economics. In the first instance, they are becoming concerned with bigger aggregates of figures. From the beginning of the Industrial Revolution the size of the productive unit has been growing—because of the advantages of specialisation of labour, because of the continued introduction of new and specialist machines capable of being operated economically only at a high rate of output, and because of expanding markets. Firms have grown progressively larger until many have control over substantial quantities of capital and are producing large and diverse outputs, for sale both at home and abroad, in complex production units. Though many small firms remain, the industrial giants of the twentieth century are tending to dominate the productive scene. The major national and international commercial concerns employ a considerable number of accountants. These men are not dealing with the personal affairs of the small trader. They are concerned with the aggregation of information to guide the policies of large business units, policies which both depend on external economic influences, and have their impact on the economic situation.

Secondly, the recording functions of accountancy are becoming progressively less important with developments in office machines. In firms of all sizes work formerly done manually is being transferred to accounting machinery. This development has two effects. Progressively less of the accountant's time needs to be spent in the aggregation of information, leaving more time available for its interpretation and utilisation. Furthermore, it is possible for accounting machines to produce aggregates which could not be provided by manual methods. The accountant both has more information to interpret and more time in which to consider it. The change in the accountant's role—from recorder to interpreter and adviser, as a result of the development of accounting machinery—is perhaps the greatest single development in accounting practice in this century.

The interpretation of financial data and the presentation of advice based on that data calls for qualities different from those one might expect to find in a record keeper. Accounting reports seldom tell the whole story about any business situation. They can be interpreted only in the context of the economic circumstances surrounding the decision process. An accountant, acting as an interpreter of financial statements with relevance to a business decision, must understand the context of the decision if his advice is to be valid. A not unlikely effect of the progress of mechanisation of record keeping is that the accountant of the future will need to know more about economics, finance, politics, and mathematics than he knows about record keeping.

Thirdly, particularly in industry, accounting is becoming less concerned with recording past events, and more concerned with forecasting future events. Management accounting techniques such as budgetary control, break-even analysis, and profit planning, though based on past record, involve forward projections, and are designed to influence the future policy and progress of the industrial unit. Looking back, and accounting for what has happened, is a matter of pure record. Forward planning is a more complex process, requiring not only the historical record which serves as the basis for future activity, but also a consideration of the means at the firm's disposal, the ends it seeks to achieve, and the methods by which the means shall be employed to achieve those ends. In this rapidly developing area, accountancy and economics become well-nigh indistinguishable.

Differences in Concepts

Although accountants and economists are concerned with the analysis of events and the formulation of policies in the same area of human activity, there are important differences in the concepts fundamental to their approaches. This is not surprising. Whilst economics modifies a general theory to meet the requirements of specific industrial problems, accountancy is a professional practice, primarily concerned with the particular affairs of individual businesses. In a sense, economists base their advice on reasoning from theory, accountants base theirs on practical experience: they approach business problems from different bases.

That the concepts of the two groups are different is not to say that they are irreconcilable, nor that the concepts of one group are invalid in the reasoning of the other. The major problem is one of understanding, of avoiding confusion through the failure of one group to appreciate the bases of the other's reasoning.

Valuation

The concept of valuation is central both to the economist's theory of the firm and to accounting practice. Yet it is in their approaches to valuation that accountants and economists differ most.

As was explained in earlier chapters, accountants usually value liquid or current assets at cost, after providing for any known inventory losses. Fixed or long-term assets are valued at unexpired cost, i.e. historical cost less depreciation provisions made. Accountants' values are factual, in the sense that they are actual prices paid for assets when they were acquired. Rarely, however, are they "realisable", "current" or "exchange" values. Thus stock is valued at cost, even when it is known to be saleable at a higher price, and plant is valued at historical cost despite the knowledge that price changes have altered both its saleable value and replacement cost. Accountants usually ignore intangible assets such as goodwill, unless they have been acquired by purchase.

To an economist, the present value of a business is the capitalised value of its expected future net earnings. Thus, if it were necessary to invest £10,000 in order to secure a future net income of £700 per year, an economist would value a business whose expected future net earnings were £1400 per year at £20,000.

This approach differs from the accountant's in several ways. In the first instance, it pays no attention to past cost. Assets only have value in so far as they contribute to future income. Secondly, it values both tangible and intangible assets alike. It might be that the future earning capacity of a business depends mainly on goodwill, in the shape of an established trade reputation, or well developed retail outlets, or some other factor. Whilst an accounting valuation would either ignore such goodwill, or would allocate to it some historic money cost, an economist's valuation would automatically include it at its present value. Thirdly, economists' valuations depend to a far greater extent than accountants' on personal judgement. Accountants' valuations are objective in the sense that they are statements of known costs. Economists' valuations are subjective in that they depend on opinions about future revenues and costs.

It is not usually claimed that the economist's approach to valuation is wrong. It is, however, generally admitted not to be accountable. What will be the future flow of income from even the most stable business must be a matter of estimation, and opinions might differ on the appropriate discounting rate to be used in calculating present value. Nevertheless, at decision points the concept is important. The prospective purchaser of a business, for instance, is unlikely to believe that adjusted historic costs represent current values, and will be decidedly interested in goodwill, whether it is recorded or not. In the last resort his offer will be conditioned by his expectations of the future profitability of the firm.

Economists generally have supported the revaluation of assets annually, or at other intervals, arguing that this would make accounting statements a more useful means of formulating judgements on business policies. Whilst this approach has been sympathetically received by many accountants, revaluation inevitably introduces a new element of estimation into valuation procedure, and accountants are usually suspicious of opinions, even where they are more relevant than the recorded facts.

In general, economists' approaches to questions of valuation are theoretically sound, but are not practical for use in financial reporting in a continuing business situation. Accountants' valuations are practical calculations, but many are theoretically questionable.

Income

The economist's concept of income follows directly from his theory of valuation. The income of a firm over a period of time is the difference between the net value of the firm's assets at the beginning and end of the period (after adjusting for any new money introduced or dividends paid out). This concept brings into income all profits whether they are realised or not, automatically adjusts for changes in the purchasing power of money, and makes no distinction between capital profits and revenue earnings. It is a valuation concept, depending solely on valuations (as previously described) at two points in time.

Accountants tend to regard the calculation of income as a matter of matching costs with revenues. Superficially, this is not far removed from the economist's approach—the difference between revenue and cost in an accounting period must be equal to the difference between the net value of the assets at the beginning and end of the period. In fact, however, there is more than a difference of emphasis here. Accounting statements of income exclude a number of items which would be included in the economist's calculation. These are:

1. *Capital items.* Because accountants do not, as a rule, revalue assets at accounting period ends, no calculations of profit or loss on holdings of durable goods are made. Even where revaluation does take place, any surplus arising is usually transferred to a capital reserve, and excluded from income statements.

2. *Intangibles.* The value of intangible assets fluctuates, but since neither the value nor the fluctuation is usually capable of quantification, it is not accounted.

3. *Changes in inventory values.* Inventories are included in accounting statements at cost, and not at saleable value. It is a rule both of accounting practice and of business prudence that profits shall not be recognised until they are realised.

As in the case of matters of valuation, the economic concept of changes in net worth is not so much incorrect, as unaccountable. Accounting measurements of income are used to support profit distributions. They are not calculations of changes in net worth, but statements of income available for appropriation to dividends or other purposes, and not all of a change in net worth is necessarily so available. In many countries there are restraints on dividends—in particular the distribution of capital profits is commonly restricted. Furthermore, the recognition of profits only when realised is a defensible proposition, even if it results in some distortion of measurement. Economists are free to learn from their mistakes, but accountants usually have to pay for theirs!

Cost

To an economist, cost usually means the value of the alternative ends which have been sacrificed in achieving the product. In determining policy a businessman selects a particular course of action from among competing claims. The cost of the product which he eventually decides to make is the value of the alternative ends to which the means could have been put. It might or might not be possible to put a money value on the economists' concept of cost in specific instances. It is a concept based on theoretical propositions about the behaviour of individuals seeking to achieve ends with limited means.

In accounting, the word cost has many different meanings. Cost statements are prepared for specific industrial purposes, and consequently on a variety of bases, yet accounting costs are almost always aggregations of the money values of factors of production required to produce a given output. This is not a matter of theory: it is a fact, a practical statement of actual resources needed to achieve an industrial objective.

It might be argued that, with regard to past events, the accountant's concept of cost and the economist's are identical. The businessman has made a decision about his objectives and has acquired factors of production for their achievement. The actual prices paid for factors of production represent their value were they applied to alternative ends. The aggregation of these prices is thus the accountant's historical cost and the economist's alternative cost. There are, however, some matters of contention.

An economist regards the cost of a product as being the value of the resources acquired specifically for its production. Thus, if the output of a firm is N units, and a decision is made to produce $N+1$ units, the cost of the additional unit is the value in exchange of the factors of production acquired to achieve the additional output. Consequently, if it were not necessary to acquire more buildings, machinery or management in order to produce the additional unit, but only materials and labour, the cost of the additional unit would be the cost of the materials and labour. This is the concept of marginal cost.

An accountant is usually inclined to take a different view, basing his reasoning on the proposition that if profits are to be made, all costs must be covered by revenue. Accountants usually include in the cost of an additional unit of output a share of the fixed costs of the business equal to that allocated to all other units. This is the concept of average cost. Thus, whilst marginal cost is:

(Cost of $N+1$) — (Cost of N units) = Cost of additional unit, average cost is:

$$\frac{\text{Cost of } N+1 \text{ units}}{N+1} = \text{Cost of additional unit.}$$

This is an area in which economics and accounting have been drawn close together. Economists have recognised that, in the long period, all costs must be covered by revenue if the business is to prosper. The relevance of the concept of average cost in considerations of this nature is accepted.

On the other hand, accountants have been turning to marginal costing in recognition of its advantages in guiding business policy, particularly in the area of short-term decision making. Unlike economists' concepts of valuation and income, the concept of marginal cost (and also that of marginal revenue) is not only valid, but also accountable. Its usefulness in management accounting practice is understood.

Towards a Greater Understanding

It has been said of accounting: [1]

"In a broad sense accounting has one primary function—facilitating the administration of economic activity. This function has two closely related phases:

(1) Measuring and arraying economic data.

(2) Communicating the results of this process to interested parties."

It is not possible to "facilitate the administration of economic activity" or to "measure and array economic data" without an appreciation of economics. Similarly, economists are "interested parties" in accounting statements, but interest requires understanding.

There is some drawing together of accountants and economists. Accountants are contributing to policy formation in large-scale industrial groups, whilst some economists are taking an interest in the activities of smaller scale economic units. Accountants are developing budgetary and forecasting techniques which are not a matter of recording, but of economic projection. In accounting records there is a rich field of statistical information available to the economist who is able to interpret it. Accountancy and economics seek to serve the same ends. They have much to contribute to each other. A greater measure of mutual understanding should be of value to both, and to others—businessmen, mathematicians and sociologists, for example, who are also concerned with solving the problems of business enterprises.

[1] W. A. Paton, *Essentials of Accounting*.

Discussion Topics

1. "Economics and Accounting, the uncongenial twins." (K. Boulding.) Are they "uncongenial", and are they "twins"?

2. Economists might be said to have traditionally taken a birds-eye view, and accountants a worms-eye view of the economy. Why is the situation changing?

3. "Bygones are bygones" to the economist, and "speculation is for the speculator" to the accountant, but are past and future events really unrelated for either?

4. " . . . the development of accounting machinery is perhaps the greatest single development in accounting practice in this century." What impact on accounting practice has the development of machinery had, and what might be the effects of the further developments which are certain to take place in the future?

5. To what extent would the adoption of revaluation techniques bring accounting measurements of capital and income nearer to the economists' concepts?

6. "It is not a question of whether accountants and economists should co-operate, they *must* if each are to make their most useful contributions to business and government." Discuss.

7. "Nevertheless, at decision points the concept (of present value) is important." Discuss.

CHAPTER 11

Politics, the Law and Accounting

ACCOUNTING concepts and procedures are not solely the product of economic demand. In many ways they are stimulated by, or suffer limitations from, political organisation and legal rules. This is to be expected. Accountancy is an interpretation of economic events, but economic events are not independent of political change, and the free operation of economic forces is commonly restricted by statutory enactments. Changing political ideas, often finding expression in legal enactments, have sometimes resulted in improvements in accounting method. In other cases, inflexible statutory rules about financial reporting have prevented development.

Political organisation varies from time to time and from country to country. In the nineteenth century government policies were mainly directed towards ensuring the utmost personal freedom of the individual in matters of trade. The general political as well as economic philosophy of the growing industrial class was that the well-being of society depended on the least interference in the private affairs of citizens consistent with the maintenance of public order. There was an accounting response to this philosophy. If the freedom of the individual in the pursuit of profit was the accepted political code, the function of accounting was to do no more than inform the directors of enterprises about the financial progress and position of their businesses.

Financial Reporting and the Law

Changing political ideas, mainly in the direction of greater state control over business affairs, have modified accounting practice. It quickly became apparent that *laissez-faire* accounting statements could be a means of perpetrating frauds on investors, and successive Companies Acts increased the amount of information which had to be revealed in the published accounts. Not only statute law but also case law had its impact on accounting concepts.

By comparison with statute law, which embraces Acts of Parliament, regulations and by-laws made under statutory authority, the term "case law" is used to refer to the law found in decisions of the courts. These decisions, which might be concerned with the interpretation of Acts, or deal with questions arising independently of statute, such as professional negligence, influence the development of accountancy in that they form a precedent for future cases involving similar problems. Legal precedents have authority not to be found in accounting practices, since a court is bound by previous decisions of superior courts and will in general follow its own earlier decisions and those of courts of equal jurisdiction. Accounting concepts, unlike legal principles, are neither prescribed nor enforced by a sovereign authority, but rather represent ideas and techniques which have gained recognition within the profession. It is only when accounting concepts are approved by the courts or embodied in statute that they become legally binding.

The case of *R. v. Lord Kylsant* [1] serves as a good illustration of how a decision of the court, by bringing to the public's notice undesirable shortcomings in accounting practice, might cause accountants to look afresh at reporting method. In this case Lord Kylsant, Chairman of the Royal Mail Steam Packet Company, and the auditor of the company were prosecuted on criminal charges on the grounds that the annual accounts and reports issued by the company were false in a material particular and were made with the intention of deceiving the shareholders. Lord Kylsant was further charged with issuing a prospectus,

[1] Fully reported and discussed in *The Royal Mail Case* by Colin Brooks—Notable British Trials series. Refer also to *R. v. Lord Kylsant* 1932 1 K.B. 442 for appeal.

inviting the public to subscribe to the issue of debenture stock, which was known to be false in that it concealed the true position of the company, with the intention of inducing persons to advance to, and invest money in, the company.

As regards the charge relating to the prospectus, the position was that the prospectus set out a statement showing that between 1911 and 1927 the company had paid dividends varying from 5% to 8% except as to one year when 4% was paid and one year when no dividend was paid. It failed to state that, for 7 years of the period involved, the company had made substantial trading losses and was able to pay dividends only by bringing in reserves created during the war. Lord Kylsant was found guilty on this charge and an appeal to the Criminal Court of Appeal was dismissed.

Both Lord Kylsant and the auditor *were found not guilty on the balance sheet charges*. Their acquittal brought home to the world at large and to the profession in particular that a state of affairs existed enabling a company to publish reports which did not show whether profits had been earned or not, and to pay dividends not from current earnings but from extraneous and non-recurring items of revenue and undisclosed secret reserves. It was clear that the law was inadequate in that it did not require balance sheets to show the full extent of reserves, or profit and loss accounts to show in detail the sources of declared profit or loss even though shareholders might be misled. Moreover, the facts of the Royal Mail Case disclosed that the auditor, who was a member of one of the largest firms of accountants in the world, had taken scrupulous care to meet all the existing legal requirements relating to audit.

As a result of the case many companies altered the form of presentation of their accounts, and showed separately items which did not represent current earnings or charges. Realising the profession's need for a "new look" in such matters, the Institute of Chartered Accountants in 1942 formed a Taxation and Financial Relations Committee to prepare a code of accounting principles. The influence this Committee had on the Cohen

Committee[1] which made recommendations prior to the introduction of Companies Act, 1948 was impressive, and reflected
credit on those involved. At the same time, the question might
well be asked whether the shortcomings in accounting reports
disclosed in the Royal Mail Case could have been avoided if the
profession at the beginning of the twentieth century had been
more active in determining and reviewing basic principles of
accountancy. That some valuable work has been done by the
professional accountancy bodies is recognised in the report of
the Jenkins Committee[2] at p.131:

> "The Recommendations on Accounting Principles periodi-
> cally issued by the Institute of Chartered Accountants in
> England and Wales to their members have already done much
> to ensure that the standards of accounting are reasonably
> uniform and constantly rising. These recommendations are
> based on close and constant study of the relevant problems,
> which are ever changing, and it is primarily to the initiative of
> the professional associations that we must look if the general
> principles of the act are to be effectively applied in practice."

That the initiative in maintaining high standards of disclosure
in published accounts rests with the profession was amply
demonstrated by the failure of the Reid Murray group of companies in Australia in 1962.[3] Reid Murray Holdings Ltd., the
parent company, had control over some two hundred companies
engaged mainly in retail trade on credit terms and in land speculation. Much of the money needed to finance the group was
raised by issues of high-interest debenture stock, and rapidly
increasing interest charges compelled the directors to pursue an
expansionist, and somewhat risky trading policy. Following

[1] *Report of the Cohen Committee,* Cmnd. 6659, (1945).
[2] A Committee set up in the United Kingdom under the Chairmanship of
Lord Jenkins to review and report upon the provisions and workings of the
Companies Act, 1948; Cmnd. 1749 (1962).
[3] The accounting implications of the failure are discussed by Professor
E. Stamp, The Reid Murray Affair, *Accountants Journal,* Wellington, May
1964, and *Accountancy*, London, August 1964.

adverse financial conditions in Australia from November 1960 the group began to experience difficulty in meeting its debt obligations, and when it finally went into receivership late in 1962 very large losses were sustained by shareholders, lenders and creditors.

From an accounting point of view, interest in the Reid Murray failure centres on the financial reports published by the Group in the years immediately prior to its failure. The published accounts of the Group for year ended 31 August 1960 showed a consolidated net profit of £1,545,340, and those for year ended 31 August 1961 a consolidated net profit of £855,616, and the balance sheet as at 31 August 1961 showed current assets of over £53 million and a working capital of over £33 million. The accounts had been audited by a recognised firm of Chartered Accountants, whose unqualified report on the 1961 accounts included the words:

> "Proper accounting records have been maintained by the company and the statements of its financial position and of its profit and loss have been properly drawn up in conformity with the provisions of the Companies Act, 1958, so as to give a true and fair view of the state of the company's affairs and of the result of its operations for the year."

It would seem incredible that a company in such apparent good health in August 1961 should be in receivership not 18 months later. Subsequent enquiry revealed that profits had been inflated by changing the basis of income recognition on credit sales transactions, that unearned income had been recognised in the profit and loss account and that, most significant of all, the provisions made for doubtful debts were quite unrealistically low.

The plain duty of an auditor is to ensure that published accounts satisfy all the requirements of the law, but to ensure that they are in accordance with the *letter* of the law is not enough. The business affairs of companies are of infinite variety, and it would not be possible, even if it were desirable, that every eventuality could be covered by statute. The general responsibility for ensuring that shareholders and other readers of published accounts are not misled rests squarely on the accountants who prepare those accounts and the auditors who audit them. As the Jenkins Committee put it: " . . . it is primarily to the initiative of the professional associations that we must look if the *general principles* of the Act are to be effectively applied in practice." [Emphasis added.]

Legal Sanctions

General responsibility for the maintenance of high standards of financial reporting thus depends primarily on the profession, but insofar as accountants must operate within the framework of the law, certain sanctions exist to secure their compliance with both statute and common law. Companies Acts, for instance, usually require auditors to make a report to the members on the accounts examined by them, and on every balance sheet, profit and loss account and all group accounts laid before the company in general meeting, and prescribe the contents of the report. An auditor might incur criminal liability for statements known to be false and wilfully made.

Quite apart from statutory duties, an auditor has duties at common law, and any attempt to contract out of such duties either under the articles of association or by contract is void. At common law an auditor is bound to exercise such reasonable care in his duties as can be expected from a reasonably competent and prudent auditor. In *Leeds Estate Building & Investment Company v. Shepherd*[1] the directors of the company were entitled to remuneration only if the dividends exceeded 5%. Without examining the books of account or the articles the auditor relied on the assurance of the manager, who had prepared false accounts so as to permit the directors to be paid, and certified the accounts as a true copy of those shown in the books of the company. The auditor was held to be negligent and liable to the

[1] [1887] 36 Ch.D. 787.

company for the loss involved in payment of remuneration out of capital.

As to the duties owed by accountants, in connection with the preparation of company accounts, to third persons, the judgement of the majority of the Court of Appeal in *Candler v. Crane Christmas and Company* [1] was until recently considered to be the law. In that case the plaintiffs desired to see the accounts of a company before deciding to invest in it. The defendants were the company's accountants, and they were told by the company to complete the company's accounts as soon as possible as they were to be shown to the plaintiff, who was a potential investor in the company. At the company's request the defendants showed the completed accounts to the plaintiff, discussed them with him, and allowed him to take a copy. The accounts had been carelessly prepared, and gave a wholly misleading picture of the state of the company. It was clear to the defendants that the plaintiff had relied on their skill and judgement, and invested money in the company which was lost when the company failed shortly afterwards. The Court of Appeal held that accountants were not liable for carelessness, as distinct from fraudulent misrepresentation, to third parties, and that they were only actionable if there was a contractual relationship.

Denning, L. J., in a strong dissenting judgement, stated:

> "Let me now be constructive and suggest the circumstances in which I say that a duty to use care in making a statement does exist apart from a contract in that behalf. First, what persons are under such duty? My answer is those persons, such as accountants, surveyors, valuers and analysts, whose profession and occupation it is to examine books, accounts, and other things, and to make reports on which other people —other than their clients—rely, in the ordinary course of business. Their duty is not merely to use care in their reports. They have also a duty to use care in their work which results in their reports."

[1] [1951] 1 All E.R. 426.

Denning, L. J., did, however, point out that it would be going too far to make accountants liable to any person who chooses to rely on their financial statements in matters of business.

The majority decision in Candler's case has now been overruled by the House of Lords in *Hedley Byrne & Co. Ltd. v. Heller & Partners Ltd.* [1] and the dissenting judgement of Denning, L. J., referred to, expressly approved. The facts in this case were that Hedley Byrne & Co., a firm of advertising agents, placed on behalf of a client, Easipower Ltd., substantial orders on credit terms for advertising time on television programmes and for space in certain newspapers on condition that Hedley Byrne & Co. became personally liable to the television and newspaper companies. Before placing the orders Hedley Byrne & Co., through their bankers, made enquiries from Heller & Partners, the bankers of Easipower, regarding the credit-worthiness of Easipower, and were given satisfactory references by a letter which was marked "confidential for your private use and without responsibility on the part of this bank or its officials". Relying on the references, which turned out not to be justified, Hedley Byrne & Co. refrained from cancelling the orders, and eventually lost over £17,000 when Easipower went into liquidation. In these circumstances Hedley Byrne & Co. sought to recover the loss from Heller & Partners on the ground that the references were given negligently, and in breach of a duty to exercise care in giving them. The claim was dismissed at first instance and appeals to the Court of Appeal and the House of Lords failed. It was held that, because Heller & Partners had expressly disclaimed responsibility for the references, they were under no duty to take care and were not liable in negligence. The decision, however, makes clear that if, in the normal course of business or professional affairs, a person seeks information or advice from another who is not under a contractual or fiduciary obligation to give it, in circumstances in which a reasonable man so asked would know that he was being trusted or that his skill or judgement was being relied on, and the person asked chooses to give the information or advice without

[1] [1963] 2 All E.R. 575.

qualifying his answer so as to show that he does not accept responsibility, then he is under a legal duty to exercise such care as the circumstances require in making his reply; and for failure to exercise that care an action for negligence will lie if damage results.

Accounting procedures are frequently the product of legal rulings. Rethinking of the profession's attitude to secret reserves and to the interests of third parties followed directly from the decisions in the cases quoted, and it is not uncommon for decided cases to compel accountants to look afresh at their reporting methods.

Taxation

The protection of investors by statutory and other legal rules has by no means been the only area of growing government interest in business affairs. The political concept of the responsibility of the state for the welfare of its citizens has developed to different degrees in different countries, but in most countries the state has become involved in providing environmental health services, education, housing and some form of social security. This, together with the heavy cost of national defence, has led to growing burdens of taxation, and particularly income taxation, which both depends upon, and exerts an influence on, accounting.

Income taxation, by its very nature, requires a measurement of income. In the interests of uniformity of application of the levy, it could not be left to individuals or business organisations to compute their incomes on whatever basis they thought best. Uniform codes of procedure for the measurement of taxable income have developed in most countries, and have had several effects on accounting practice, some beneficial, some not.

1. Many more people keep adequate records of their financial affairs because of taxation rules than would otherwise be the case. Sole traders and partnerships have frequently employed accountants not because they appreciated at the

outset the value of accurate records for their own sake, but solely because of the need to submit taxation returns. Taxation legislation has both encouraged better record keeping in small firms, and given a stimulus to the growth of the accountancy profession.

2. Taxation rules, on the other hand, have retarded the development of accounting procedures and the general adoption of advanced methods. Even more tenaciously than accountants, tax officers cling to objective measurements of value, to historic costs (particularly as the basis for depreciation allowances), and to the "matching" process of income calculation. Whilst it is neither uncommon nor improper for firms to prepare their tax returns on bases quite different from the more appropriate bases used in the construction of their own accounts, there is a tendency, especially in smaller businesses, to allow inflexible taxation rules to influence thought on internal matters of income measurement and asset valuation.

The Relationship between Accountants and Lawyers

To separate the functions of lawyers and accountants is not a simple matter, since the fields overlap and each case must ultimately be considered in the light of its own particular circumstances. The important point is that both lawyers and accountants should be well qualified and the public be left to select the particular service it requires.

P. B. Temm[1] considers that in tax matters the accountant's role should be to work with the lawyer on matters of accounting, while the lawyer should advise on the law of taxation in the light of all the legal principles affecting the case. The best relationship between accountants and lawyers, where they practice in related fields, might be for the case to be prepared by the accountant and the lawyer in collaboration and for the lawyer to appear in court

[1] P. B. Temm, The [legal] profession and the future years, *New Zealand Law Journal*, No. 5, March 1964, p.106 (new series).

with the accountant as his witness. The opportunity for team work seems great, while the field for conflict is small. Very often a financial problem can be properly solved only if both professions make a contribution. Dean Erwin Griswold considered the tax practice controversy in America in 1955 and stated: [1]

"For the most part, the tax lawyers of my acquaintance have had very good relations with accountants, have had great respect for the work they do, and have often worked with them on many kinds of matters as a very effective team with great mutual respect. Most lawyers have worked on a good many matters which they could not have handled, or could not have handled as well without the aid of a good accountant. The accountants associated with them on these matters were quick to recognise that they could not have handled some aspects of the matter as well as the lawyer did. By my observation there are few things as satisfying to a lawyer in tax practice as working closely with a good accountant, seeing him develop materials better than you did, seeing him pick up one of your ideas and putting it into graphic form, tying it into the facts of the case—or on the other hand, having the accountant present data on which the lawyer is able to build up a legal argument beyond what the accountant was prepared to contribute."

In 1951 a statement of principles relating to practice in the field of federal income taxation was agreed upon and was approved by the House of Delegates of the American Bar Association and by the Council of the American Institute of Certified Public Accountants. It was considered that lawyers should encourage their clients to seek the advice of accountants whenever accounting problems arose, and accountants should encourage clients to seek advice of lawyers whenever legal questions were raised. That conformity with this principle might result in the employment of two persons rather than one is not of great consequence, since

[1] Reprinted in *The Journal of Accountancy*, vol. 99, 1955, p.36.

if the questions are sufficiently important, the services may well be justified.

As the structure of modern business becomes more complex, the professions must complement each other, and live and work together on a basis of mutual accommodation and esteem. The ideal relationship between accountants and lawyers could well be, as expressed by Magruder: [1]

"In the contiguous areas where conflict may arise, both professions must serve a new profession—business—like two boys tied together in a three-legged race; the success or failure of one is dependent on that of the other."

Accounting without Profit

Certainly the most important area in which political events have shaped, or sometimes mis-shaped, accounting practice has been the growing field of economic activity under the control of the state, either directly or by the use of state agencies. From their traditional responsibilities for defence and the maintenance of law and order, governments have extended their interests into many and diverse economic affairs.

Only rarely do central governments maintain accounts on double-entry principles. They do not usually keep asset accounts, or provide for depreciation, nor do they distinguish capital and revenue transactions. Consequently there is no clear distinction between current operating costs and capital formation. In effect the published accounts of governments are statements of cash received from loans, taxes and other sources, and disbursements made, the balance being either an overspending or an underspending.

Following the Municipal Corporations Act 1882 (U.K.), accounting without profit found a fresh field of expression—local government. From the beginning, local authorities kept their books on double-entry principles, but the basic concept of their

[1] *Handbook of Modern Accounting Theory*, edited by Morton Backer, p.95.

accounting statements is one of stewardship over public money. Revenue accounts are records of the income received from government grants and local taxes, and the expenditure of income on the provision of local services. Balance sheets are historic statements of sources of capital finance (usually government or local loans or contributions from revenue) and the expenditure of money on long-term assets.

The chief criticism of governmental and municipal accounting is that, lacking the necessity to measure profit, it has remained content to compare cash flows. The overriding consideration in matters of government finance is not so much what was raised and what spent, as was expenditure effective? Though both government and municipal tax levies are based on detailed budgeting, inadequate attention has been paid to the analysis of variations of actual productivity and expenditure from budgeted levels. The accounts of the state and its agencies would be of considerably more value if they were phrased in terms of objectives planned at costs estimated, as compared with objectives achieved and actual expense incurred.

It was perhaps a reaction from the cash accounting procedures of governments (though there might have been other reasons) which impelled the British Government during the nationalisation "spree" following the 1945 election to provide in most of the nationalising statutes that the new public authorities should prepare their accounts "in accordance with the best *commercial* standards". [1] Accounting forms resulted which showed the "profit" or "loss" of each authority for each financial year. Since, however, the authorities were appointed wholly by, and were responsible to, the government, and since they were each endowed with an absolute monopoly (except to the limited extent they compete with each other, e.g. Gas versus Electricity), the terms "profit" or "loss" mean little more than "tax" and "subsidy". That electricity commonly makes profits is no cause for rejoicing: it merely means that consumers of electricity pay more for the services they receive than those services cost. Similarly, the early

[1] See, for example, S.50 of the Gas Act, 1948.

losses incurred by the Coal Boards can only be interpreted as subsidies to coal users (among whom are the profitable gas and electricity industries).

Accounting methods of governments, municipalities and state agencies have been determined by political ideas, often framed in legislative rules. By no means always, however, has the result been the most appropriate or meaningful type of accounting reporting. Accounting is a device by which information is communicated, and accounting reports should be so framed as to be a guide to informed thought about economic processes. The effect of both company legislation and case law has been to increase the amount of information available in the published accounts of limited companies, and to make that information more meaningful to investors. No such endeavours have been made in the public sector. Neither historic statements of cash flows nor calculations of state agencies' "profits" and "losses" provide adequate material for debate on issues of public policy.

Politics, Law and Accounting

Political and legal influences on accounting during the past century have had a confused effect. Sometimes they have resulted in the rethinking of erroneous or undesirable accounting ideas, and often they have caused more and more useful information to be prepared and published. On the other hand, some enactments have led to the introduction of inappropriate reporting methods, and much legislation has restricted progress in accounting.

It should not be necessary for political and legal forces to compel accountants to provide adequate and useful information in published statements, nor should accountants be content with legally enforced but inappropriate reporting forms. The task of so shaping accounting method that reports are beyond the reproach of the courts, yet meaningful in their economic and political context, lies not with governments or lawyers, but with the accountancy profession. There remains much to be done before the ideal is achieved. [1]

Discussion Topics

1. How might the legally unregulated published financial accounts of the early limited companies have been a means of perpetrating frauds on investors?

2. "The Royal Mail Case did not alter the law on financial reporting, but it revolutionised the attitude of the accountancy profession and the business community at large on the question of disclosure of information in published accounts." Discuss.

3. Were the auditors of the Reid Murray Group justified in attaching an unqualified report to the accounts of the Group dated 31 August 1961? In what ways might they have qualified their report, and what might have been the effects of a qualified report?

4. Can it be said that the only real safeguard for the investor in a public company is an alert and honest accountancy profession, and that the best the law can do is to strengthen the authority of the auditor?

5. The judgement in the Hedley Byrne Case has been described as "more than uncomfortable for the profession". Why?

6. "Income tax laws have improved the accounting procedures of small firms, worsened those of medium-sized firms, and had little effect on those of large firms." How might this be the case?

7. Is it desirable for a socially owned organisation to keep accounting records and present financial reports "in accordance with the best commercial standards"?

[1] Part of this chapter is based on an article by Eric Freeman LL.B.; *Accountants Journal,* Wellington, October 1964.

CHAPTER 12

The Utility of Accounting Statements

ACCOUNTING is a communications art, a means by which one person conveys information about an entity, or part of an entity, or a past or projected future activity of an entity to another person or a group of persons. Accounting reports are almost always condensations of a mass of statistical data, generated by the activities of the entity, into classified aggregates capable of comprehension by the recipients of the reports. As has been indicated in earlier chapters, there is no single process of accounting equally applicable in all circumstances to all entities, and no single short series of financial reports can satisfy the information requirements of all the people who are interested in the activities of the entity. Distortion is almost inevitable between reality and the report; the structure of classification is arbitrary, and there are alternative assumptions about the valuation of factors of production and the allocation of costs against revenues. It might be said that the object of accounting theory is the isolation of the factors which cause distortion in accounting reports, the measurement of the extent of that distortion, and the discovery of procedures that will minimise the difference between the reality of the entity and its activities and the depiction of the entity and its activities in accounting reports.

Internal Financial Reporting

The greater part of accounting activity is directed towards providing information for managers, of all levels, of entities, to assist in the day-to-day control over factors of production, in decision formation and the development of policy. Internal financial reports need not be concerned with the whole of an entity, they might focus attention on a department, a product, a process or some other subdivision. Nor need they, or should they, be confined to financial information contained in ledger accounts; statistical data in other than money terms is often as pertinent in factor control and decision formation. There are many texts on the technology of management accounting, but underlying all are the assumptions:

1. *An internal accounting report must be specific to its purpose.* External financial reports have to serve many purposes for diverse groups of people, but each internal report has a single objective—to give information on a specified matter to a known person or persons. There is thus no need for generalities in internal financial reports, each can be "custom built" for the job it is intended to do.

2. *There must be identity of understanding among all parties to the report.* Cost, value, process and other words commonly used in reports are capable of various definitions. In this context two things are important: the definitions chosen must be the most appropriate to the purpose of the report, and what definitions have been chosen must be known not only to the constructor of the report but also to all recipients. An accounting report can be more misleading than helpful if the basis of its construction is not fully understood by all who use it.

3. *Accounting reports must be integrated into the control and planning processes of the entity.* Lack of integration can result in mis-use or under-use of accounting data, and this is not uncommon. To some extent this is the fault of industrial accountants who are often content to remain in their offices churning out periodic cost reports without due concern as to whether they are appropriate to the present productive processes of the entity, or whether they are correctly used or indeed used at all by the recipients.

If reports are to make their impact on events, the accountant responsible for their construction must fully comprehend those events, and if this is to be so, not only the reports *but also the accountants* must be integrated into the processes of the entity. Equally at fault are often managers of all kinds, who do not ask for the reports they need, or who fail to use the reports they get because of lack of understanding. There is often a need in industry for executives to be trained in the use of numerical data, and equally a need for account-ants to keep abreast with the development of the entity's business. Accounting is a management tool, but it is unlikely to be useful if it is the wrong tool for the job or if the ways in which it can be used are not understood.

4. *If accounting reports are to have their due impact on events, they must be timely.* Accountants sometimes have an obses-sion with arithmetical precision which, having regard to the wide areas of discretion in accounting measurements, is difficult to understand. The control of production, if it is to be effective, depends on immediate, and not historic data, and decisions cannot usually be delayed until calculations have been perfected to the last penny or the nth decimal point. A report right to within £1000 now is likely to be much more use to a manager than one right to a penny 3 months hence.

External Financial Reports

External financial reports usually have to deal with the entity as a whole, and to describe events over a fixed time-period, usually one year, and depict the position of the entity at the period-end. They are used by a variety of people, shareholders, long- and short-term creditors, stock markets and the general public, with diverse interests, and it is difficult, if not impossible, to serve the information needs of all in a single series of published accounts. It is not unusual that the published accounts of a company do no more than give inferences about its progress and financial position.

X.Y.Z. Co. Ltd.

Income Account for year ended 31 March 02

	Year 01 £	Year 01 £	Year 02 £	Year 02 £
SALES		640,000		680,000
Less Purchases	400,000		420,000	
+opening stock	40,000		60,000	
	440,000		480,000	
—Closing stock	60,000	380,000	70,000	410,000
GROSS PROFIT		260,000		270,000
Less Administration	70,000		75,000	
Selling costs	50,000		60,000	
Directors' fees	50,000		55,000	
Depreciation	20,000	190,000	20,000	210,000
NET PROFIT		70,000		60,000
Add Undistributed Profits b/fwd.		50,000		40,000
		120,000		100,000
Less Transfer to special reserve for increased replacement costs	30,000			
Dividends paid	50,000	80,000		50,000
BALANCE carried to next year		40,000		50,000

X.Y.Z. Co. Ltd.

Balance Sheet as at 31 March 02

	Year 01 £	Year 01 £	Year 02 £	Year 02 £
FIXED ASSETS:				
Freehold land		50,000		50,000
Building (at cost)	400,000		410,000	
Less Aggregate provision for depreciation	60,000	340,000	70,000	340,000
Machinery (at cost)	110,000		130,000	
Less Aggregate provision for depreciation	50,000	60,000	60,000	70,000
		450,000		460,000

GOODWILL at cost		100,000	100,000
TRADE INVESTMENTS at cost		50,000	50,000
(Market value at balance date)	(64,000)		(67,000)
NET CURRENT ASSETS (WORKING CAPITAL):			
Stock (at cost)	60,000		70,000
Debtors	60,000		70,000
Cash	10,000		5000
	130,000		145,000
Less Creditors	40,000	90,000	55,000	90,000
		690,000	700,000

Financed from:			
SHAREHOLDERS' FUNDS:			
500,000 shares of £1 each		500,000	500,000
RESERVES:			
General	20,000		20,000
Special reserve for increased replacement costs	30,000		30,000
Unappropriated profits	40,000	90,000	50,000	100,000
		590,000	600,000
BANK LOAN		100,000	100,000
		690,000	700,000

A useful supplementary statement is one which traces the funds which became available to the company during the year back to their sources, and demonstrates the manner in which the company disposed of those funds. Thus:

X.Y.Z. Co. Ltd.
*Source and Disposition of Funds
for year ended* 31 *March* 02

	Year 01 £	Year 02 £
FUNDS PROVIDED		
Net income	70,000	60,000
Non-cash expenditure included in the computation of net income—depreciation provision	20,000	20,000
	90,000	80,000

FUNDS APPLIED

Cash dividends paid	50,000	50,000
Increase in fixed assets	20,000	30,000
Increase in working capital	20,000	—
	90,000	80,000

	Year 01 £	Year 02 £

CHANGE IN WORKING CAPITAL:

INCREASES

Increase in cash balances	5000	—
Increase in value of stock held	10,000	10,000
Increase in debtors' balances	15,000	10,000
	30,000	20,000

DECREASES

Reduction in cash balances	—	5000
Increase in creditors' balances	10,000	15,000
	10,000	20,000
Net increase in working capital	20,000	—
	30,000	20,000

Statements of the sources and disposition of funds serve to link balance sheets at two period-ends together, and throw some additional light on the financial policy of the company.

Accounting Ratios

Some things are obvious from a superficial inspection of the accounts; the company is maintaining its sales volume and making profits, but is nevertheless short of liquid assets, and particularly cash. A more penetrating analysis is possible with the aid of ratios, of which the commonest used are as follows:

1. *Gross Profits: Turnover*

Year 01
£260,000: £640,000
or 0·406: 1

Year 02
£270,000: £680,000
or 0·397: 1

An alternative, and often more useful way of expressing the same thing is to say that in Years 01 and 02 respectively, 40·6% and 39·7% of each £ of sales was available for administrative and other non-trading expenses and profit.

Ratios are not usually useful as absolute statistics. They have value only when related to other information. Some trades have a generally high ratio of gross profit to sales, others have a low one: it depends on the kind of product, the productive methods employed, and market conditions. Whether or not the X.Y.Z. Co.'s ratio is satisfactory depends on what is reasonable having regard to the business it does.

The change in the ratio from Year 01 to 02 is interesting, and serves to stimulate further enquiry. The worsening position might be due to changing purchase costs or selling prices, or some combination of these factors, or to differences in inventory valuations, or other circumstances.

2. *Average Value of Stock: Cost of Sales* (Stock turn)

Year 01	Year 02
£50,000: £380,000	£65,000: £410,000
or 0·132: 1	or 0·159: 1

Once again, the calculation raises interesting questions. In Year 02 relatively higher values of stocks were held. This might be due to any one of several factors, or a combination of some. For instance, the company might be diversifying its sales pattern, thus requiring the stocking of a greater number of types of goods. Alternatively, the difference might be monetary—the same quantities of stock might be in hand but the method of valuation changed. Again, it might be that some element of the stock is proving difficult to sell.

An alternative way of expressing this ratio is to say that in Year 01 the stock was "turned over" 38/5 times, or 7·6 times, or about once every 7 to 8 weeks. (The figures for Year 02 are 410/65, or 6·3, or every 8 to 9 weeks.)

As was the case with gross profit margins, the appropriate ratio of stocks of raw materials and work in progress to cost of sales varies from trade to trade. In some industries, particularly those with a long production cycle (e.g. shipbuilding), it is high. In others, where the production cycle is short (e.g. in fisheries), it is low. Whether X.Y.Z. Co. Ltd.'s ratio is satisfactory or not depends on the kind of business it does.

3. *Net Profit: Proprietors' Capital Invested*

Year 01	Year 02
£70,000: £590,000	£60,000: £600,000
or 0·119: 1	or 0·100: 1

Alternatively, the business might be said to be earning a return on capital invested of 11·9% in Year 01 and 10% in Year 02. Whether or not this is reasonable depends mainly on the degree of risk involved in investment in the kind of business the company does.

The declining rate of return on capital invested merits investigation. It could be due to any of a multitude of factors—changes in costs of factors of production, in selling prices, in trading methods or administrative organisation are some examples.

4. *Current Assets: Current Liabilities*

Year 01	Year 02
£130,000: £40,000	£145,000: £55,000
or 3·25: 1	or 2·64: 1

This ratio demonstrates the extent to which the company's position is liquid. It is a measure of the company's ability to continue to pay its way in current trading transactions. The fall in the ratio, and the smallness of the cash element in current assets should lead to questions about the saleability of stock and the reliability of debtors, since these factors will obviously be significant in the short-term finance of the company's business. A useful supplementary measure, particularly for firms with a slow stock turnover, is the "quick assets ratio"—debtors plus cash and readily saleable securities: current liabilities.

The value of debtors can be further explored by the ratio:

5. *Debtors: Credit Sales* (Age of Debtors)
        (All X.Y.Z. Co. Ltd.'s sales are assumed to be credit.)

Year 01	Year 02
£60,000: £640,000	£70,000: £680,000
or 1: 10·6	or 1: 9·7

A more useful way of expressing this ratio is to calculate the average period of credit allowed to debtors:

Year 01

$$\frac{52}{10\cdot6} = 4\cdot9 \text{ weeks}$$

Year 02

$$\frac{52}{9\cdot7} = 5\cdot4 \text{ weeks}$$

This is to say that (assuming £60,000 to be the average value of debtors in Year 01) the debtors paid for their sales in 10·6 "instalments", and that the period between "instalments" of 4·9 weeks is the average period of credit allowed.

That the average period elapsing between sales and the receipt of cash is rising might be due to extended terms of credit being allowed as a matter of sales policy, or to inadequate efforts to secure collection, or to poor credit control, resulting in the creation of bad debts. It is a matter worthy of investigation.

6. *Other Ratios*

The usefulness of ratios in the analysis of accounts depends on the purpose of the investigation and the nature of the accounts. Other ratios sometimes used are Fixed Costs: Total Costs (particularly in manufacturing businesses) and Creditors: Purchases (dealt with in much the same way as Debtors: Credit Sales described above). Ratio analysis is useful in showing relationships between statistics and in revealing areas where further inquiry about the company's affairs might prove worth while. In a practical situation, figures for more than 2 years would be needed to give an adequate picture of financial trends.

Limitations of Financial Statements and Ratio Analysis

Financial statements deal with one aspect only of the structure of a firm: its monetary results and position. This is an important aspect, but there are always other factors to be considered. A statement is of more practical use if read in conjunction with other relevant information, about the efficiency of the firm's management, the quality and age of its plant and equipment, its present and potential market, sources of supply of productive factors, and development plans, for example.

This proposition was illustrated in the discussion of ratios. What is a reasonable return on capital or a reasonable inventory level for a particular firm depends on matters not disclosed in the accounts, chiefly the nature of the product made, the degree of investment risk involved and the type of productive process used. Similarly, whilst changes in accountancy ratios from one period to another might be of interest, they are surface expressions of more fundamental phenomena.

A more important deficiency of financial statements stems from the discussion in Chapter 9. Traditional practice is to value fixed assets at historic cost, less provisions for depreciation made, and current assets at the lower of cost or realisable value and this might invalidate the statements altogether as guides to action. To illustrate this point, one of the commonest ratios described in accounting texts is the "proprietorship ratio", i.e. Shareholders' Funds: Tangible Assets. For X.Y.Z. Co. Ltd. [1]

Year 01	Year 02
£590,000: £630,000	£600,000: £655,000
or 0·94: 1	or 0·92: 1

This ratio is supposed to reveal the extent to which the shareholders have controlling ownership of the company. In fact, however:

---

[1] Tangible assets are:

	Year 01 £	Year 02 £
Fixed assets	450,000	460,000
Investments	50,000	50,000
Current assets	130,000	145,000
	630,000	655,000

1. The figure is high because, in Year 01 (e.g.) outside sources of finance of £140,000 (bank loan £100,000, creditors £40,000) are largely offset by excluding goodwill (because it is not "tangible") at £100,000 from the assets.
2. The calculation is based on historic, and maybe quite unrealistic values for fixed assets. The buildings might be of small value, or considerable value, but there is no reason to suppose that, because they *cost* £340,000, they are worth £340,000, whatever is meant by "worth" (e.g. realisable value, replacement cost or value to the business as a going concern). The same might be said of the land and the machinery.
3. Goodwill is excluded from the calculation altogether. It might, in fact, be worthless, in which case it ought not to appear in the accounts at all, but if it does appear in the accounts it should be included in the calculation at its present value. To do anything else renders the ratio meaningless.

The proprietorship ratio is of little use except when valuations realistic in the light of expected future action can be allocated to assets, e.g. break-up values if the firm is to be wound up, or aggregate saleable value if transfer of control is intended.

Though to a lesser extent, the same sorts of problem are associated with other accountancy ratios. For instance, even if consistent methods of valuation are used, the ratios Gross Profits: Turnover and Average Value of Stock: Purchase Cost of Sales will differ according to what is meant by "cost" of stock— LIFO or FIFO based, direct cost, absorption cost, or some other system of valuation. Similarly, Net Profit:Proprietors' Capital Invested is a purely monetary measure, a comparison of profits in current £s with investments and reserves made in £s of past periods. If, in Year 01, the directors of X.Y.Z. Co. Ltd. had not chosen to create a special reserve for "increased replacement costs" but had written £30,000 off the value of fixed assets as additional depreciation, a different ratio would have resulted.

Financial accounts depend not only on facts, but also on opinions and policy decisions. They can be interpreted only in the light of full information, which though it should be available to a substantial potential investor on enquiry, is not usually made generally available.

Published Company Accounts

Even with the assistance of supplementary information it is difficult for the fairly complete reports which have been illustrated to be interpreted to any effect. The accounts published by limited companies under statutory requirements present even greater problems, partly because supplementary information is not usually available and partly because less detail is disclosed. The amount of information which must be given in annual published company statements varies somewhat from country to country, but typical requirements are:

1. Every balance sheet of a company shall give a true and fair view of the state of affairs of the company at the end of its financial year, and every profit and loss account of a company shall give a true and fair view of the profit or loss of the company for the financial year.
2. Information on directors' emoluments, including pensions and compensation for loss of office must be revealed, also any loans made to officers of the company.
3. The profit and loss account must show:
   (a) turnover, classified by product groups,
   (b) the amount charged for depreciation,
   (c) interest on debentures or other fixed loans,
   (d) amounts transferred to or from reserve,
   (e) income from investments,
   (f) dividends paid and proposed,
   (g) exceptional or non-recurrent profits or losses or profits or losses which have arisen because of a change in the basis of accounting,

      (h) comparative figures for the previous year.
4. The balance sheet must show:
      (a) the authorised and issued share capital of the business,
      (b) assets and liabilities, summarised to show their general nature, and classified under headings appropriate to the company's business,
      (c) fixed assets, distinguished from current assets, shown at cost or a valuation less aggregate depreciation written off. The method used to arrive at the amount of the fixed assets in each class must be stated,
      (d) capital reserves, revenue reserves and provisions under separate headings,
      (e) the aggregate amount of the company's investments, distinguishing trade investments and quoted and unquoted other investments and the aggregate market value of quoted investments,
      (f) the value of goodwill or other intangible assets as shown in the books of the company,
      (g) any special security relating to a liability of the company,
      (h) comparative figures for the previous year.

These provisions are fairly comprehensive, but they carefully avoid requiring the company to reveal matters which might be of interest to trade competitors. For instance:

1. No information need be provided about purchases, manufacturing expenses or administrative costs (except directors' emoluments).
2. Current assets need not be analysed into inventories, debtors and cash.
3. Aggregate amounts only need be provided in many cases.

Not only trade competitors would be interested in such information, but also the company's shareholders and prospective shareholders, and other investors. Whilst legal provisions probably protect the public from the more obvious forms of fraud by company directors, they require that published accounts be little more than a brief statement of net profit, transfers to and from reserves, dividends declared and proposed, and asset and liability aggregates on a basis of historical cost (or valuation).

A "True and Fair View"

The overriding provision of company legislation in some countries is that accounts shall present a "true and fair view" of the profit or loss and the financial position of a company. This is an advance on previous provisions, which required only that accounts be "correct". Both companies and accountants tended to interpret the word "correct" in the narrow arithmetic sense of "in accordance with a correct set of double-entry accounts". The concepts of truth and fairness obviously demand a broader approach. They are, however, concepts lacking precision of definition.

In the first instance, a statement of assets valued at historic cost is surely true. Every figure quoted is a fact, an actual money payment made for an asset at some previous point in time. But if money values have changed, or there are important alterations in the production or trading circumstances of the firm, the statement might not be fair. On the other hand, if assets are revalued to current prices, the asset list might be fair, but would only be true in the sense that it is a representation of someone's opinion. A valuation might be true but not fair, or fair but not true. The choice between objective measurement and subjective valuation is an invidious one.

The same sort of proposition holds good with regard to profit measurement. Whilst stocks are valued at cost or lower, and depreciation provisions are tied to historic cost, profit measurements are true in the purely accounting sense. Yet, because the value of inventories might be well above cost and because depreciation provisions might be adequate or less than adequate to maintain productive capacity, the measurement might not be fair. On the other hand, to revalue inventories at selling price would be to anticipate profits not realised, and to adjust depreciation rates to replacement values would involve subjective judgement. A fair statement of profit might only be true in the special sense that it is someone's opinion of truth.

Another dimension of the problem is that published accounts are primarily prepared for the information of shareholders. They are legally the directors' report of their stewardship of the shareholders' investment. Yet other people are involved—prospective investors, debenture holders and other long-term creditors, short-term creditors and the general public. What might be either a true or a fair statement with regard to one class of people might be less true or less fair with regard to another. American practice is to state in audit reports that accounts have been constructed in accordance with Generally Accepted Accounting Principles, and this is probably preferable to the use of the words "true and fair".

The Basic Accounting Problem

The insistence on historic cost valuation of assets, the refusal to anticipate profits before they are realised, and the disinclination to accord values to intangible assets are deeply embedded in accountancy practice. Accountants have been concerned to limit their measurements to observable facts, and to avoid elements of judgements as far as possible in accounting statements. To a large extent this approach has been encouraged by statutory enactments, aimed mainly at protecting the money investments of shareholders. Truth, in the objective sense of monetary measurement, has been the keynote, rather than fairness, in the sense of subjective valuation.

As a result of this long-established tradition it is becoming questioned if accounting statements are anything more than interesting to those who understand the basis on which they are constructed, and if they might not be positively misleading to people without such understanding. The question which remains unresolved is that of whether accountants will remain content to be financial historians, or whether they will essay into the less secure areas of judgement and opinion in an attempt to make their statements more meaningful.

Discussion Topics

1. What are the basic requisites for the effective use of accounting in the management of business enterprises?

2. Mr. A: "Accounting reports would be easier to understand if they were not so full of jargon." Mr. B: "One of the advantages of accounting is that it does not need a special technical language. All the words used have well-known meanings in common usage." Mr. C: "Accountants not only attach technical meanings to words, they are not averse to giving the same word several meanings if it suits their purpose." They couldn't all be right, could they?

3. How could an accountant be *integrated* into a business organisation, and if he is employed by the firm, could he possibly not be integrated?

4. "A more penetrating analysis is possible with the aid of ratios." Is it?

5. What effect might the assumptions made about inventory valuation, the valuation of long-term assets and the matching of costs and revenues have on ratio analysis?

6. What do you understand by the term "a true and fair view"? Did the accounts of the Royal Mail Co. in 1927 and those of the Reid Murray Group in 1961 give a "true and fair view"?

7. "As a result of . . . long-established tradition it is becoming questioned if accounting statements are anything more than interesting to those who understand the basis on which they are constructed, and if they might not be positively misleading to people without such understanding." Discuss.

8. "The question which remains unresolved is that of whether accountants will remain content to be financial historians, or whether they will essay into the less secure areas of judgement and opinion in an attempt to make their statements more meaningful." Discuss.

APPENDICES

A. Double-entry

B. The Literature of Accounting

APPENDIX A

Double-entry

Introductory students of accounting frequently find it difficult to grasp the basic idea of Pacioli's theory, and their studies of accounting are thereby retarded.

For the benefit of such students, an elementary interpretation of double-entry principles is appended.

IT TAKES two to make a bargain: every sale involves a purchaser; every debtor has his creditor; for every borrower there is a lender. The general proposition, which stems from legal rights in property, that there must be at least two parties to a commercial transaction, is an obvious one. What is perhaps less obvious is that there are two aspects to every commercial transaction for each of the contracting parties. Thus, if A sells goods to B for cash, A has both parted with goods and received money, whilst B has paid money and acquired goods. This is equally the case if A sells goods to B on credit. In these circumstances A loses the goods but acquires B as his debtor, whilst B obtains possession of the goods but must acknowledge A as his creditor. The basic concept of double-entry, as Pacioli saw it, and as we see it today, is that for each individual business there are two aspects to every commercial transaction it undertakes. The double recording of transactions is not mere duplication of effort; it is the adjustment of the books so that both of these aspects are accounted.

An alternative way of looking at the double-entry principle is to regard a business as a collection of assets and liabilities. In the ordinary course of trade, assets are not given away, nor are liabilities incurred without recompense. Assets are exchanged for other assets, goods and services are exchanged for money, and liabilities are incurred in exchange for value received. Each commercial transaction thus results in two changes in the asset and liability structure of a business. Double-entry is accounting for both of the changes in the structure of the business which result from each trading action.

There are, in general terms, four ways in which the assets and liabilities of a business might change as a result of a commercial transaction. These are:

(a) *Acquisition of assets*. Assets are means at the disposal of firms for the pursuit of business aims. They are acquired by receiving cash, goods, or other tangible things like machinery and plant, and obtaining claims to assets such as debtors or company shares. Using the services of employees and organisations such as banks, insurance companies and transportation firms is another form of asset acquisition. Although these assets take the form of services rather than commodities, they are essential for the conduct of all businesses.

(b) *Disposal of liabilities*. Liabilities are claims by persons outside the firm on the firm's assets. They are disposed of when creditors of all kinds, ranging from ordinary trade creditors to long-term mortgage holders, are repaid: that is to say when claims on the firm's assets are extinguished.

(c) *Acquisition of liabilities*. Liabilities to other firms or persons might be acquired in the ordinary course of trade when purchases are made on credit, or, less usually, by borrowing from banks or other lenders, or by hire purchase or other special borrowing agreements.

(d) *Disposal of assets*. Assets are disposed of when goods are despatched to purchasers, when cash is paid out, when machinery or other long-term assets are sold or scrapped, or when debtors repay.

The usual process of trade is that when assets are acquired (a), or liabilities are disposed of (b), this is in exchange either for the acquisition of liabilities (c), or the disposal of assets (d). In simple terms, commercial transactions, viewed from the standpoint of one business, consist of the exchange of (a) and/or (b) for (c) and/or (d).

In conventional accounting, categories (a) and (b) are collectively described as debit aspects of transactions, and are entered on the left-hand side of accounting forms, whilst categories (c) and (d) are collectively called credit aspects, and are entered on the right-hand side of accounting forms.

The operation of the double-entry system in the books of a trader, A, might be illustrated in journal form as follows:

(1) *A buys goods on credit from B for* £100
    Debit purchase of goods account (a)   £100
        Credit B's account (c)   £100
(2) *Goods worth £20 prove to be unsuitable and are returned to B*
    Debit B's account (b)   £20
        Credit returned goods account (d)   £20
(3) *A pays B £50*
    Debit B's account (b)   £50
        Credit cash account (d)   £50

Because both aspects of each of these transactions has been recorded in the books of A, a complete account of the position of A's business has been kept. Thus the purchase of goods account reveals that £100 worth of goods have been acquired and, taken together with the returned goods account, it is known that £80 worth of these goods are still in the possession of A. B's account reveals that £30 is still owing to him. The cash account shows that £50 has been paid out of the business.

Proprietor's Capital

It is accounting practice to regard the assets and liabilities of a business as being entirely separate from the private estate or estates of its owner or owners. Consequently, when a proprietor invests capital in a business, by placing money or goods at its disposal, the investment is regarded in the books of the business as an acquisition of assets (i.e. the money or goods) counter-balanced by the acquisition of a liability—the liability of the business to its proprietor for the capital he has invested. In effect

proprietors are regarded as a special type of creditor. This is not
unreasonable. Proprietors do not usually invest in businesses
unless they expect at some date that their capital will be returned.
Investment by a proprietor, whether a sole-trader, or a partner,
or a shareholder in a company, is regarded as a special case of
the acquisition of a liability in the business books. Thus, if A
invests £200 in cash in the business which has been used as an
illustration above, the book-keeping entry would be:

Debit cash account (a)	£200	
Credit A's capital account (c)		£200

Trial Balances

The principal purpose of double-entry is the comprehensive
recording of each aspect of every transaction. There is, however,
an important secondary advantage. Since there are two aspects
to each transaction and since these aspects are recorded, one on
the debit side and the other on the credit side of an account in the
ledger, it follows that the total debit postings must at any point
of time equal the total credit postings.

Thus the total debit and credit postings illustrated are:

	Debit £	Credit £
Purchase of goods account	100	
Returned goods account		20
Cash	200	50
B's account	70	100
A's capital account		200
	370	370

The procedure of adding the accounts in a ledger and proving
the equality of the debit and credit sides in total is known as
"trial balance". It is a useful test of the accuracy of accounting
for transactions since, if an item has been posted in debit only, or
has been posted twice on the debit side instead of once on each
side of the accounts, the trial balance will not agree. Though a

check on the accuracy of accounting, it should be noted that the trial balance is not an infallible proof. If a transaction has been posted at an equal, though incorrect, figure, both to the debit and to the credit of accounts in the ledger, the books will be in error, yet the trial balance will not reveal it. Similarly, if an item has been posted in the correct amount but to the wrong account, the mistake will not be shown by the trial balance. Obviously, if a transaction has not been recorded in the books at all, the trial balance will not reveal the omission.

The usefulness of the trial balance as a proof of the ledger has been recognised since Pacioli's day. Early practice, however, was often to trial balance the ledger only when the pages were full and the accounts were being transferred to a new book. Modern accounting method is to trial balance the ledger at the end of each accounting period, and very often at intermediate dates, so that errors might be located quickly and corrected.

Account Balances

Balancing is the process of setting off debits against credits in each account in the ledger, to reveal the net effect of transactions recorded. Thus, A's cash account has a debit entry of £200 and a credit entry of £50. After setting off one against the other, a net debit balance of £150 remains. In B's account there are debits for £20 and £50 and a credit for £100. The net credit balance is £30.

Modern practice is to balance accounts frequently. Accounts with creditors and debtors are usually balanced monthly, so that bills can be sent out and payments made, and other accounts are balanced at varying intervals according to the frequency with which the proprietor needs to know the net position on the account. Quite often accounts are balanced daily, and some modern accounting systems provide for the balancing of accounts every time a new transaction is entered.

It might be noted that the balancing of accounts simplifies but does not disturb the equality of the two sides of a trial balance. Thus, after account balancing, the trial balance already illustrated reads:

	Debit £	Credit £
Purchase of goods account	100	
Returned goods account		20
Cash	150	
B's account		30
A's capital account		200
	250	250

The Concept of Profit

Although each transaction has two aspects and, since both are recorded in the ledger, a constant state of balance must be maintained, it by no means follows that the business remains in a state of stagnant equilibrium. Businesses are run for profit, and the usual process of making profit is to sell goods for more than was paid for them. Thus, when A bought his goods from B, the net effect of the book-keeping entry was:

Debit purchase of goods account (a)	£100	
Credit returned goods account (d)		£20
Credit B's account (c)		£80

The goods now remaining in A's possession cost him £80. Should he now sell them to C for £120, the book-keeping entry would be:

Debit C's account (a)	£120	
Credit sale of goods account (d)		£120

Quite plainly, because A has sold goods for more than he paid for them, he has made a profit. Yet the books remain in equilibrium.

Profit arises when assets acquired in one commercial transaction are disposed of at a higher price in another. Conversely, loss takes place when goods are sold for less than they cost. The fundamental equation:

$$\begin{array}{c} \text{Assets acquired (a)} \\ + \\ \text{Liabilities disposed of (b)} \end{array} = \begin{array}{c} \text{Liabilities acquired (c)} \\ + \\ \text{Assets disposed of (d)} \end{array}$$

is in neither case disturbed.

The Income or Profit and Loss Account [1]

At the end of an accounting period it is possible to distinguish two kinds of account appearing in the ledger. In the first category are all those accounts which record assets still in the possession of the business or liabilities still owed by the business at the balancing date. Examples of such assets are cash, machinery and debtors, whilst continuing liabilities are creditors of all kinds and the proprietor's capital.

The second category of accounts is that which contains records of transactions which have been completed during the accounting period. Purchases and sales of goods accounts, returned goods accounts and expense accounts fall in this class.

In the case of A's business, as it has been illustrated, the continuing accounts, i.e. the asset and liability accounts remaining at the end of the accounting period are:

	Debit	Credit
	£	£
Cash	150	
B's account		30
C's account	120	
A's capital account		200

The accounts recording transactions completed during the period are:

	Debit	Credit
	£	£
Purchases of goods account	100	
Returned goods account		20
Sale of goods account		120

As will be observed, A's ledger "trial balances"—both the total debit balances and the total credit balances amount to £370.

All entries in the terminating accounts are now transferred to the profit and loss account in the following form:

[1] The names are alternative.

A's BUSINESS

Profit and Loss Account for the period ended . . .

	£		£
DEBITS		CREDITS	
Purchases of goods	100	Returned goods	20
		Sales of goods	120
	100		140
PROFIT—i.e. surplus of credits over debits, transferred to A's capital account	40		
	140		140

The Balance Sheet

The accounts which terminate during an accounting period are closed to the profit and loss account, so that income might be calculated, and to clear out of the ledger records of transactions which are now complete.

The remaining, continuing accounts are carried forward, since they represent not only assets and liabilities existing at the end of one accounting period, but also those with which the business will begin the next.

At the end of each accounting period, continuing balances are exhibited on a balance sheet. In A's case, the balance sheet would read:

A's BUSINESS

Balance Sheet as at . . .

	£		£
CREDITS		DEBITS	
A's capital account	200		
Add Profits	40		
	240		
B's account	30	C's account	120
		Cash account	150
	270		270

It is traditional practice in Britain to show credits on the left-hand side, and debits on the right-hand side of a balance sheet, contrary to their position in the books of account. In other countries, notably in America, debits are shown on the left and credits on the right. Alternatively, the balance sheet might be presented in the form of a continuous narrative. For example:

A's BUSINESS

Balance Sheet as at . . .

	£	£
ASSETS		
C's account	120	
Cash	150	270
	—	
Less LIABILITIES		
B's account		30
		—
PROPRIETOR'S INTEREST		
A's capital	200	
Plus profits	40	240
	—	—

The balance sheet is not an account. Whilst the income account is a dynamic statement dealing with transactions which have taken place over a period of time; a balance sheet is static, describing the position of a business on a given date, in so far as it is revealed by the accounting records.

In that the balance sheet lists continuing accounts going forward from one accounting period to another, it provides the opening entries for the accounting period beginning on the balance date.

APPENDIX B

The Literature of Accounting

AFTER the pioneer work of the early writers, books on accountancy appeared in considerable numbers. There is today no shortage of material either on the general principles of the subject or its special applications. Both the growth of interest in accounting and the development of the profession have, however, produced accounting periodicals. Reflecting, as they do, contemporary practice of, and thought on, accounting matters, they are worthy of some comment. It might well be said that, whilst the early ideas of accounting found their expression in books, modern developments are more likely to appear first in the periodical literature.

Accounting Journals

The earliest regular journal was the *Accountant*, which has been published in London since 1874. Unlike most accounting periodicals, the *Accountant* is not the official organ of a professional body. Appearing weekly, and with a large and international circulation, the *Accountant* might properly be described as the profession's "newspaper". It has proved to be the vehicle for many new ideas in accountancy, for much controversial writing, and for not a little unimaginative conservatism in its long history. No doubt it will continue to cater for all tastes in the future.

Less exciting, more authoritative, and usually more conservative are the official organs of the professional bodies. Among the leading publications, *Accountancy*, the journal of the Institute of Chartered Accountants in England and Wales began its career in 1889, the Scottish Chartered Accountants' *Accountants Magazine* in 1896, the American Institute of Certified Public Accountants' *Journal of Accountancy* has appeared since 1906; the *Chartered Accountant* and the *Australian Accountant* in Australia since 1901 and 1936 respectively, and in New Zealand the *Accountants Journal* has been published since 1922. All are published, usually at a financial loss, by professional societies, for the exchange of accounting ideas, for the discussion of developments, to publicise professional activities and policies, and to provide a link between members and their professional organisations. Most have regular contributions for student readers.

In 1925 there appeared the first edition of the *Accounting Review*, published by the American Accounting Association. [1] The *Accounting Review,* which has appeared regularly since that date, is significant because it is a vehicle of academic and not professional opinion. More often more theoretical than practical, speculative rather than descriptive, and written by scholars rather than practitioners, its contribution to the literature of accountancy is invaluable. Not tied to meeting the everyday technical needs of professional men, nor to presenting the policies of any professional group, it has frequently been the inspiration for developments, through writing which could not have found expression in the ordinary professional journals. *Accounting Research*, which appeared in Britain in 1948, had similar aims, but it ceased publication in 1958. In 1963 the *Journal of Accounting Research* sponsored jointly by the London School of Economics and the University of Chicago and in 1965 *Abacus*, an Australasian academic journal, began new ventures in accounting scholarship.

Research Series

Research series, which have been published by some professional bodies, fall into three classes. First are series which seek

[1] The American Accounting Association is not a professional body, but an organisation of university teachers of accounting, and others interested in academic debate about accounting.

to publicise best known accounting and reporting methods with a view to encouraging their adoption by practising accountants. The English Chartered Accountants publish *Recommendations on Accounting Principles* and the Institutes in Australia and New Zealand issue modified versions of the English recommendations, as well as recommendations of their own, from time to time. The American Institute of Certified Public Accountants similarly has produced bulletins on auditing procedure, terminology, accounting principles, and other subjects.

There is no doubt that these considered opinions on best current accounting practice have had a considerable impact. Practitioners, by and large, have adopted the procedures recommended, in preference to generally less desirable alternatives. (In some instances their adoption has been made mandatory on members of the profession.) Not infrequently recommendations have been incorporated in statute law when, for example, revisions of the Companies Acts have taken place. The general effect of recommendations on accounting practice has been to improve and standardise accounting method, especially in the field of professional practice.

A second group of publications by professional bodies has been aimed at informing accountants of new developments. There have been many volumes of this kind, dealing with subjects as diverse as taxation, farm management accounting, the automation of data-processing procedures, accounting for small unincorporated societies and the management of professional practices. Though advisory rather than mandatory, they make a most useful contribution to the literature of practical accounting, and are invaluable to the accountant dealing with the varied problems of business administration.

Perhaps most interesting of the research series, and, indeed, probably the only ones deserving the title of "research", are those which seek to establish basic principles of accounting, or to resolve difficult problems of practice. Several professional bodies have made efforts in this direction, but the leading series is the *Accounting Research Studies* published by the American Institute of Certified Public Accountants. This series makes searching enquiry into some of the problems touched on in this volume: for instance, the basic postulates of accounting, accounting principles for business enterprises, and accounting for the effects of price level changes. Others have been concerned with particular problems of accountancy—cash flow analysis and funds statements, reporting of leases in financial statements, and accounting for business combinations.

Textbooks are basic in the programme of education in accounting: they are condensations of the wealth of thought and experience of the past. But accounting does not live in the past, and the student or practitioner who ignores the periodical literature and research series cannot have more than an imperfect understanding of his subject as a living part of modern business.

Further Reading on Accounting Theory

This book is not more than an introduction to the theory and context of accounting. There is much more to learn, and many issues remain controversial. The following reading list is not comprehensive. It is intended as no more than a guide to further reading in one of the most exciting areas of accounting thought.

ASSOCIATION OF CERTIFIED AND CORPORATE ACCOUNTANTS, *Accounting for Inflation*, London, Gee & Co., 1952.

BACKER (Ed.), *Handbook of Modern Accounting Theory*, Prentice-Hall, New York, 1955.

BAXTER and DAVIDSON (Eds.), *Studies in Accounting Theory*, 2nd edn., Sweet & Maxwell, London, 1962.

BRAY, *Four Essays in Accounting Theory*, Oxford University Press, 1953.

CANNING, *The Economics of Accountancy*, Ronald Press, New York, 1927.

CHAMBERS, *Accounting and Action*, Law Book Co., Sydney, 1957.

EDEY, YAMEY and THOMPSON, *Accounting in England and Scotland 1543–1800*, Sweet & Maxwell, London, 1963.

EDWARDS, *History of Public Accounting in the United States*, Michigan State University, 1960.

EDWARDS and BELL, *Theory and Measurement of Business Income*, University of California Press, 1961.

EDWARDS and SALMONSON (Ed.), *Contributions of Four Accounting Pioneers— Kohler, Littleton, May, Paton*, Michigan State University, 1961.

GILMAN, *Accounting Concepts of Profit,* New York, 1945.

GYNTHER, *Accounting for Price-Level Changes: Theory and Procedures,* Pergamon Press, Oxford, 1966.

JONES, *Effects of Price-Level Changes on Business Income, Capital and Taxes,* American Accounting Association, 1956.

LADD, *Contemporary Corporate Accounting and the Public,* Irwin, Homewood, Ill., 1963.

LITTLETON, *Structure of Accounting Theory,* American Accounting Association, 1953.

LITTLETON, *Accounting Evolution to* 1900, American Institute Publishing Company, New York, 1933.

LITTLETON and YAMEY, *Studies in the History of Accounting,* Sweet & Maxwell, London, 1956.

LITTLETON and ZIMMERMAN, *Accounting Theory—Continuity and Change,* Prentice-Hall, Englewood Cliffs, 1962.

MAUTZ and SHARAF, *The Philosophy of Auditing,* American Accounting Association, 1961.

MAY, *Twenty-five Years of Accounting Responsibility* 1911–1936, American Institute Publishing Company, New York, 1936.

MAY, *Financial Accounting,* Macmillan, New York, 1943.

NORRIS, *Accounting Theory,* Pitman, London, 1946.

PATON, *Accounting Theory,* A.S.P. Accounting Studies Press.

PATTON and LITTLETON, *Introduction to Corporate Accounting Standards,* American Accounting Association, 1948.

PERAGALLO, *The Origin and Evolution of Double Entry Book-keeping,* A.I.C.P.A., New York, 1938.

PRINCE, *Extension of the Boundaries of Accounting Theory,* South-Western Publishing Company, Cincinnati, 1963.

SCHMALENBACH, *Dynamic Accounting* (translation by Murphy and Most), Gee & Co., London, 1959.

STACEY, *English Accountancy—a Study in Social and Economic History* 1800–1954, Gee & Co., London, 1954.

STAUBUS, *A Theory of Accounting to Investors,* University of California, 1961.

VATTER, *The Fund Theory of Accounting and its Implications for Financial Reports,* Chicago University Press, 1951.

ZEFF and KELLER, *Financial Accounting Theory,* McGraw-Hill, New York, 1964.

Index